12/06
80

ﬁen

abandon ship!

abandon ship!

HAL BUTLER

Henry Regnery Company · Chicago

Library of Congress Cataloging in Publication Data

Butler, Hal.
　Abandon ship!

　1. Shipwrecks.　　I. Title
G525.B94　　　910'.453　　　74-6886
ISBN 0-8092-9024-3

Published by Henry Regnery Company
114 West Illinois Street
Chicago, Illinois 60610
Manufactured in the United States of America
Library of Congress Catalog Card Number: 74-6886
International Standard Book Number: 0-8092-9024-3

Contents

Introduction

W<small>HENEVER</small> the subject of disaster at sea is discussed, the first two examples that come to mind are the sinkings of the *Titanic* and the *Lusitania*, the classic sea tragedies of all time. The loss of life alone—1,517 on the iceberg-shattered *Titanic* and 1,198 on the torpedoed *Lusitania*—is enough to give them a special niche in the annals of the sea.

But ever since man first put a primitive raft in water, catastrophies of all kinds have pursued him. Men have fought the forces of nature, fire, and collision damage to keep their fragile crafts afloat. Sometimes they were successful, other times not.

The continuous drama of men against the sea has fascinated not only mariners but landlubbers who have never been closer to the sea than a swim at Miami Beach. some perverse manner, shipwrecks with great loss of are always singled out as the most exciting and spec lar. But loss of life alone is not the only criterion for measuring drama on the waters of the world. The element of drama is present in the captain who stubbornly stays with his sinking ship; in a dangerous rescue mission that succeeds, or even fails, in the face of great obstacles; in the bravery, or the cowardice, of men under stress; and in the lone survivor's tale of endurance and frustration.

In this book I have not included the *Titanic* or the *Lusitania*, since their stories have been told so often, but have related the stories of some lesser-known ship disasters—some that the reader will remember, some that he won't. I hope the book will provide interesting reading and, perhaps, give you a better understanding of ships and the men who sail them.

Hal Butler

1

The *Negociator*:
Only One Survived (1809)*

T HE nor'wester struck in the early morning
of November 25, 1809, lashing the brig *Negociator* with
heavy snow and sleet. All through the day the 150-ton
sailing vessel, out of Philadelphia on a sealing mission,
inched her way through a murky tempest, dipping and
rolling in the roughest weather she had yet encountered.

By midnight, moving slowly under shortened sail, she
was shrouded with an ominous mantle of ice. But the ice
that clothed the ship was not what worried her tense
twenty-one-man crew. For almost a month the
Negociator had picked her way, with the cautious hesi-
tancy of a blind man, through a field of giant icebergs.
Now, buffeted by a strong northwest gale, she was in

---

*Originally published by *Argosy* magazine, Popular Publications, September, 1959.

1

imminent danger of smashing herself to bits against the tumbling mountains of ice.

Daniel Foss stood spread-legged on the slippery fo'c's'le deck, his body braced against the howling fury of the nor'wester. His eyes searched the soupy darkness as he tried to spot, in time to sound a warning, any ice mountain that might suddenly loom off the bow. A rugged, hard-bitten, and experienced seaman, he knew full well the peril in which the *Negociator* journeyed. She had come a great distance since leaving Philadelphia, shaping her course for the Friendly Islands and then into the northern Pacific where the waters were dotted with danger. Now, on the very edge of the sealing waters, it seemed impossible to Foss that she could founder in heavy seas or be broken like an eggshell against a wall of ice.

James Nicoll, master of the ship, skidded across the rolling deck and grasped Foss' arm. "Look sharp, mate!" he said grimly. "If you spot a berg ahead, split your lungs!"

Foss nodded. "If we hit one on the weather side in this high sea," he replied, "we can count our minutes."

The words were prophetic. At exactly two-thirty in the morning, a grinding, scraping noise rumbled up from the bowels of the ship and the *Negociator* shuddered like a wounded monster. The brig had hit an old growler—an almost submerged iceberg—and the ice island had ripped the belly out of the ship!

Foss stumbled and scrambled awkwardly trying to maintain his balance on the slanted deck. Already it was obvious that the *Negociator* was doomed, and in the blackness of the night he saw men struggling to get provisions, and themselves, into the longboat. By the time he reached it, most of the crew were already seated.

Master Nicoll stood in the stern and his voice sang out above the hissing noise of the storm. "Lower away!" he shouted. "Lower away, there, damn it!"

The longboat rattled down the sides of the listing *Negociator* and dropped with a hollow splash into the turbulent green-blue sea. Desperately the men took to the oars, pulling out from under the ship's lee. Five minutes later, crowded together in the open boat, Foss and twenty other frightened men watched the stricken ship quietly slip beneath the waves.

Dawn found the men huddled miserably in the longboat, their faces red-raw from the icy wind, their teeth chattering. None were equipped to cope with the frigid weather. They had scrambled into the longboat with such haste that some had no jackets, and several were even barefooted.

As soon as dawn brightened the sky, Master Nicoll took stock of what provisions they had. There were fifty pounds of beef, half a barrel of pork, a barrel of water and a keg of beer. Nicoll ordered the men to lift a small sail into place and then faced the worried crew.

"God knows we don't have enough food for a long spell," he said, "but we'll ration what we have equally. And we'll take turns rowing and bailing the boat. Our only hope is to make our way south to a warmer climate, or we die in this weather."

The *Negociator* had been in the field of icebergs for almost a month. Reaching a warmer climate in an open boat would take at least seven toilsome weeks. It was a hopeless and impossible task.

It was now January twentieth, eight long weeks since the sinking of the *Negociator*, and the tiny longboat lay becalmed on a mirror-like expanse of still blue water. In

the east, a saffron sun rode the rim of the world like a ship
afire on the horizon, then exploded upward to vault across
the unbroken water that was the mid-Pacific.

There were only three survivors left.

Foss, sitting in the stern, rubbed his bearded face as he
gazed dully at his companions. One was Master Nicoll,
the other a seaman named Jones who had served as
surgeon on the *Negociator*. The rest, eighteen in number,
had perished.

Foss, recalling the bitter cold and intense suffering
they had endured during the eight terrible weeks in the
longboat, counted it a miracle that three still lived. But
now, having reached the milder climate they had sought,
a new and even more frightful specter haunted them.
They had just consumed the last of their food. Only a
small amount of fresh water remained. And the sun had
become an implacable enemy that would scorch, burn,
and ultimately destroy them.

"Somewhere in this damned ocean there must be an
island," said Nicoll desperately.

"Somewhere there is," agreed Foss bitterly and lapsed
into morbid silence. In the pit of his stomach was the
grinding ache of near-starvation, for, like the others, he
had not eaten adequately since the demise of the
Negociator.

Foss looked at his companions and wondered who
would be the first one to go. He was convinced that none
of them could last more than two days.

But five days and five nights passed, with the relentless
heat of the sun parching their throats and searing their
skins during the day and the chill of the cool air freezing
them at night, and still they lived. The hunger pains grew
more insistent and, in an effort to lessen them, the men
cut their shoes into small bits, softened the tough leather
in the remaining fresh water, and chewed it with the

plodding patience of the famished. At last, on the fifth day, Master Nicoll made the suggestion all three of them had been dreading.

"We're not going to get through, mates—not all of us anyway," he said thickly. "It's a hard thing to say, but if any of us are to survive, one must be sacrificed and eaten."

Foss stared blankly at Nicoll. He had expected this, but he did not like it. He rebelled at the thought of cannibalism. Yet for weeks he had considered the possibility that it might come to this. The thought of eating human flesh twisted his stomach, but he recognized the necessity of it and he was persuaded to cut three strips from his shirt, one marked with a brown thread, and place the strips in a cap from which they would draw lots.

Conversation stopped as each drew forth a piece of cloth with trembling hands. They looked at each other a long moment, then each revealed his draw. Surgeon Jones had picked the fatal piece.

Jones sucked in his breath, steadied himself with an effort, and at last spoke. "I have a wife and three children in Norfolk, Virginia," he said hoarsely. "I make only one request—that if either of you ever get home you let my family know what happened." Then the doomed man dropped to his knees in the bottom of the boat, and his lips moved in silent prayer.

When he was finished, he extended his left arm. "Cut the vein," he said simply.

Foss reached for his knife, but the weapon trembled in his hand. He looked at Nicoll, who turned away.

"Scared of a little blood, are ye?" scoffed Jones, forcing a grin. "Here—allow me."

He took the knife, and with one deft movement severed the large vein. Blood gushed from the wound, and Foss and Nicoll stared at it in horror.

"Drink it!" demanded Jones impatiently. "Don't let it go to waste. Drink, damn both of ye!"

Nicoll, like a savage animal, grabbed Jones' arm and pressed his mouth to the wound, drinking the blood as it poured forth. Then Foss, hunger cancelling out normal reluctance, drank from the wound.

For the next twelve days Foss and Nicoll lived on Jones' body, which they sliced carefully and dried in the sun. Fortunately, rain supplied them with fresh water, which they caught by wringing their wet clothes into the bucket used for bailing the boat. But the loathsome food provided only slight nourishment. In those twelve days both men weakened noticeably, growing too feeble to stand on their own legs in the longboat. At last even this terrible food was gone, and Foss and Nicoll, now reduced to hollow-eyed skeletons, were convinced that death was only hours away.

But on the very day that they ate the last of Jones' body, they spotted on the southwest horizon a thin strip of land. The sight so electrified them that they took to the oars, summoning energy they were not aware they had, and rowed toward it. By the next morning they found themselves approaching an island, which they estimated must be about two miles in circumference.

The sight of land was welcome but there was a discouraging aspect, too. The island was bordered by high, craggy rocks against which the sea broke with a thunderous roar. To their dismay, they found that there was not a spot where they could attempt a landing with any guarantee of safety.

Nevertheless, they agreed to try it. It was about four-thirty in the afternoon, and the sun was setting. Cautiously the two men rowed the boat toward the craggy rock-studded coast, and as they neared the island, the surf became angry and turbulent. About one hundred yards from the shore a giant wave suddenly lifted the boat completely out of the water, flipping it over like a pancake on a griddle. Foss, grabbing one of the huge twenty-foot oars, was thrown clear, into the raging surf. He was a good swimmer, and the mammoth oar helped to buoy him. He splashed frantically as another swell carried him at breakneck speed toward the sharp, projecting rocks. He scrambled up beyond the grasp of the thundering waves, and sat exhausted, scanning the broken shoreline. He saw nothing but the shattered fragments of the longboat, smashed into unbelievable slivers by the waves. Nicoll was gone.

It was almost dusk before Foss regained sufficient strength to explore the island. In the gathering darkness he stumbled on unsteady legs across sand and rock, searching for edible plants or springs of fresh water. With each step he grew more discouraged. It seemed that he had landed on an island that was totally incapable of supporting human life!

A half-mile long and about a quarter of a mile wide, the place was completely barren—not a tree, a blade of grass, a bit of foliage, not even a stick of driftwood anywhere. Misshapen rocks were piled grotesquely about as if spread by the hand of a careless giant. All else was sand.

There was no evidence that the island had ever been visited by man. No seagulls hovered over it; no animals or insects crawled its surface. In the hollows of several rocks, Foss found rain water, but it was brackish and unfit to drink. As night closed in, he located a shallow cave near the shore and lay down in it, completely fatigued and discouraged. This was truly an island devoid of all food, and even the prospect of catching fish off the shore was hopeless because of the treacherous waves and his weakened condition.

With a night's rest, perhaps he would be strong enough

to explore his island domain more thoroughly the next day. Then, if he found no food, he would have to accept the terrible truth—that this weird and desolate sandbar would become his deathbed.

Foss did not sleep that night. He lay on his back, staring into the pressing blackness, appalled at the insoluble problem that confronted him. About midnight rain began to fall in large drops. To quench his terrible thirst, Foss crawled from his cave and lay on his back outside, catching the precious drops in his mouth as they fell. But the shower lasted only a few minutes.

Toward morning he dozed briefly, and when he awoke he was wet with perspiration. Already the sun was high in the sky, smothering the island in oppressive heat. Foss found he could hardly push himself erect, and when he stood up he wobbled unsteadily. But still he covered the entire island, inch by incredible inch. It took most of the day, and when he was finished he knew beyond doubt that there was nothing there but sand and rock. He had seen no living thing, no plant or animal.

Just before darkness, he crawled back into his shallow cave. Despite the fact that he had lost weight during his ordeal and was now little more than a skeleton, he noticed with some alarm that his legs and arms had begun to swell. He tried to remember what he had heard or read about starvation.

All that night he lay in a half-sleep while his mind spun with delirious thoughts of his home and parents. When morning came, to his surprise, he was still alive.

He set out once more on his hopeless search for food and water. He found, this morning, that he was even weaker than the previous day. It was necessary for him to crawl over the burning sand and rock much of the way, resting for long intervals.

His search was as futile as it had been the day before—
until late in the afternoon, when he stumbled upon a
thing that, at least temporarily, would stave off death.

Near the pounding surf, he found a cavity in a rock that
held the remnants of a dead seal. For a moment he could
hardly believe his eyes. He knew, by the fetid odor and
appearance of the seal, that it was in a putrid state, but this
did not keep him from eating it. He fell on the meat
ravenously, hardly chewing it in his frantic anxiety to get
it into his pain-riddled stomach. But then he realized the
harm that gorging himself would do, and he gathered up
the remaining meat and carried it to his cave.

That night he awoke with chills racking his body. His
face was flushed with fever, his tongue swollen, his throat
and mouth cotton-dry. As he lay, ill and dazed, a strange
sound, like the staccato barking of dogs, drifted through
his consciousness. He knew that such a sound on this
silent, tomb-like island was an impossibility, and he
wondered with some alarm if he might be delirious.

When morning came he remembered it. Had the barking been real or had his mind been playing tricks on him?
He decided to force himself to investigate.

He had difficulty getting to his feet, but he finally
emerged from his cave on wavering legs—and stared with
red-rimmed eyes. What he saw made his heart jump with
excitement. Literally thousands of seals were perched
on the rocks and shelves of the shore! It had been their
barking he had heard!

His heart pounding with anticipation, Foss grabbed the
only weapon, other than a small knife, that he had—the
oar he had rescued from the longboat. Gathering all his
remaining strength he staggered into the mass of seals,
swinging the oar right and left in savage arcs. The seals,
surprised by this sudden mayhem, took the blows almost

without moving. To his delight Foss found that a blow to the head of a seal with the oar was sufficient to stun and sometimes kill it.

For almost three hours, he stood in the midst of the stunned beasts, felling them with the oar. Then at last, the creatures realized what was happening and, as if on signal from a leader, disappeared into the sea. By that time, more than a hundred seals lay dead and dying on the rocky beach. Foss dropped to his knees, exhausted, and lay among the stricken beasts for most of the morning before he could regain enough strength to start cutting and gathering the meat.

The job of cutting the seals into strips and drying the meat on the rocks took Foss several weeks of continuous labor. But the meat afforded him nourishment, and the sickening blood from the creatures substituted, at least temporarily, for water. He gradually began to feel stronger, and when, at last, he had cached his supply of meat in his cave, he knew for the first time that the specter of starvation had been removed. There remained only the problem of obtaining and storing sufficient water.

With his strength increasing daily, Foss decided to clean out all shallow rock formations to catch rain water when the rains finally came. Then he arranged smaller rocks over the shallow basins in such a way as to shut out both salt spray and the rays of the sun.

Within a few days, a steady rain came that filled the basins and provided him with enough water to last indefinitely.

With the problem of food and drink solved, Foss' existence on the island entered a new phase—the long pull that would either find him victorious over his environment or reduced to a jibbering madman. It was obvious by now that he had landed on an island off the beaten path of navigators, and he held slim hope that he would ever be rescued. He was faced with the problem of living in complete loneliness, looking at the same unchanging horizon, seeing the same sand and rocks, for year after endless year. Under such conditions, unless he had something to occupy his mind and time, he would inevitably go insane.

He decided to build himself a house. The idea excited him, and he went to work at once. Selecting the highest point on the island for his home, he began to carry rocks to the pinnacle. It turned out to be back-breaking work. For four weeks he labored under the hot, strength-sapping sun, carrying and rolling and shoving the rocks to the summit of his lookout point, on several occasions almost dropping in his tracks from sheer exhaustion. At the end of four weeks, he had completed a crude but livable stone shelter.

With his house finished, time began to weigh heavily for him. Day after day, he sat miserably lonely. In some amazement he watched his beard grow until it was six inches long. After a time it became matted and tangled, and the hair on his head grew long and cushioned the back of his neck from the sun. His skin became dried and withered under the incessant sun, and his body, dressed in ragged clothing, resembled that of a scarecrow.

He decided that he should have some means of reckoning time. But how to keep a calendar? He had no paper, no pen, no ink. Using his knife, he scraped the broad end of the oar and carved notches in it to represent days. Every seventh day he counted a Sunday, and gave thanks on that morning by chanting an appropriate hymn.

One day, while sitting in emptiness before his stone hut, he decided to carve the words of the hymn on the oar. It was a laborious and monotonous job. It took him an entire day to carve a dozen tiny letters and several weeks to complete the hymn.

He was living exclusively on uncooked seal meat and water. He grew tired of the fishy taste of the seal, but it was all he had. From time to time the seals returned to the island, and when they did he killed more of them, cut them, dried them, and added them to his cache. The rains came more frequently, too, filling his basins and potholes with precious water.

Week after week and month after month passed. Then finally a year was gone, during which Foss had occupied himself by making vessels for holding his water. This was accomplished by the incredible method of grinding hard stones into softer hollow ones to make shallow basins. It took five weeks to complete just one such vessel.

Since his clothes were becoming more and more tattered, Foss also set about making himself a complete suit from seal skins. This didn't prove very successful, however, because the skins grew dry and hard, and Foss could wear them only for short intervals before they began to chafe his body.

At the end of the first year he decided to erect a tower on his island high point, hoping that any passing vessel might see it. In an entire year he had not once seen a ship, but he felt he must do something. Stone by stone, the beacon rose, and on top of its thirty-foot height, he placed a flag made from his waistcoat. In the second year, he erected a wall twenty feet square and ten feet in height around his hut, for no reason except that it quickened the passage of time.

During the third year, there was little to do but keep track of the time by notching the oar, and occasionally to kill a few seals to add to his food supply. During idle times he found himself pacing along the beach, back and forth, like a caged animal. Often—because he felt the silence might drive him mad—he would talk to himself, and was surprised to find that his voice, so seldom used, had become a hoarse croak.

Once, in June of the third year, he spied a sail passing to leeward. But it was too far away and he could not attract the attention of the passing ship. Yet the sight of it was enough to keep his hope for eventual rescue throbbingly alive.

It was not until March of the fourth year that Foss experienced a change in the sameness of the days—and then he was not sure that he welcomed it. One night at about nine o'clock, as nearly as he could reckon it, a violent hurricane struck the island. He had known some severe blows in his life as a seaman, but nothing to equal this. A howling wind and driving rain smashed across the defenseless island from the southwest, while thunder and lightning crackled savagely overhead. But, despite the fact that the huge waves, driven by the hurricane, completely inundated the lower sections of the island, Foss' house on the pinnacle remained above water.

By morning, the storm had dissipated itself and Foss climbed down from his lookout to see what damage had occurred. To his surprise he found little, since the island was made only of sand and rock, and most of this had remained in place. In fact, the hurricane had actually brought him a bonanza, for he found the rocks along the shore covered with flying fish, washed up by the storm. In half an hour, he gathered enough to replenish his food stock, when he crossed to the southwest shore of the island to see what might be there. To his amazement he found an enormous whale washed up on shore—and in its lifeless body was a harpoon with several fathoms of new line attached.

The discovery encouraged Foss, for the harpoon in the whale meant that whalers might be operating nearby. But his optimism gradually diminished as the fourth year passed without any sign of a ship on the horizon. Yet every morning he ascended a few steps to the base of the beacon he had built and gazed out to sea, hoping to see a ship.

Since his varied provisions now included seal meat, flying fish, and whale steaks—enough food for a year— Foss busied himself inscribing upon the oar some of the more memorable incidents that had happened since he had been stranded on the sand bar. By this time his hopes of rescue were at low ebb, and he had decided to set down for posterity a record of his fate.

The fourth year passed. Then, near the end of his fifth year on the island, Foss became ill and for two days did not make his morning pilgrimage to his lookout. Ironically, this lapse in his daily routine almost cost him his chance to be rescued.

Although he felt little better on the third day of his illness, something induced him to trudge to his lookout point. The sight that met his eyes was unbelievable. Like a man stunned, he stood looking at it for a long time. A ship, with topsails aback, was anchored just off the island!

Foss, forgetting the sickness in him, suddenly went berserk, jumping from rock to rock, waving his cap in the air to attract attention. At last he saw the master of the ship, at the taffrail, adjust a spyglass to his eye. His heart leaped painfully in his chest. He had been seen!

The master of the ship made a gesture with his hand, and Foss saw for the first time that a longboat with three men in it was attempting to land. Seizing his prized oar, he ran down on the beach toward the spot where the boat was trying to land.

As he came to the edge of the water, he saw one of the men in the boat make a hopeless motion with his hands to indicate that they could not land.

Foss cried out in anguish. Still grasping the oar, he plunged recklessly into the foaming surf and struck out for the boat.

At once he realized the foolhardiness of the move. A giant swell roared in and pushed him back to shore, almost impaling him on a jagged rock. But he was determined, and again he dove into the water. This time he made some progress before the next swell pushed him back again, but he kept on swimming, fighting the huge waves, using the huge oar to buoy him, battling the sea with all the strength left in him. The men in the longboat watched him in amazement and at last, swimming and thrashing violently, he reached the boat and was helped aboard.

The ship proved to be the *Neptune*, bound from Batavia to New Bedford, Massachusetts. Her master was Captain Call, a bearded patriarch in the finest tradition of sea captains.

When Foss had been taken to the captain's quarters and placed upon a soft bed, Captain Call asked question after question, and when Foss told him how long he had been on the desolate island the old sea captain refused to believe it.

"You're a better man than Robinson Crusoe, to hear you tell it," he scoffed. "Out, now, with the truth of it!"

Wearily, Foss pointed to his oar. "A calendar of my stay," he said weakly. "Each day recorded with a notch."

Captain Call examined the carved oar in amazement. After a few more questions he became convinced that Foss told the truth. "It's an ill wind that blows no one good luck," he said at last. "The *Neptune* has been far off her course because of contrary winds; otherwise we would never have seen this island. It shows on no map or chart. And we would have passed it by, even so, had I not spied your signal of distress."

Foss' first meal aboard the *Neptune* was an indescribable delight. But so ingrained was his habit of storing everything edible, against famine on the island, that when the *Neptune* finally reached New Bedford, sailors found pieces of meat and bread craftily hidden in his cabin.

It was not, however, until after Foss was rescued that the most curious part of his fabulous story was revealed. For two weeks before he was cast adrift when the *Negociator* sank, he had spent every moment he could spare from his duties reading a book in which he had become completely absorbed.

It was Defoe's *Robinson Crusoe*.

2

The *Polly*:
Derelict to Nowhere (1811)

THE captain stood at the taffrail of the brig *Fame* and adjusted the long, tapering spyglass to his eye. Alongside him the first mate, squinting against the glare of the sun, said, "A derelict. That's what she is, sir."

The captain nodded. He could see the ghostly hulk quite clearly now—a dismasted brig, floating low in the water, her warped and sun-dried decks barely visible above the rolling blue sea. Twisting the spyglass to bring the derelict into sharper focus, his jaw dropped at the sight that met his eyes.

"I see two men aboard her!" he said excitedly. "One stands at the rail, waving. The other is sitting on the hatchway coaming. He seems to be crying. Both of them look like living skeletons!"

Passing the spyglass to the first mate, the captain raised his brass trumpet to his lips. "Ahoy, there! Captain Featherstone of the *Fame* here! Who are you?"

The emaciated figure at the rail stopped waving, staggered drunkenly a moment, then collapsed to the deck. The weeping man buried his face deeper in his hands, and his shoulders rocked with emotion.

There was no response from the derelict. . . .

In the disaster-filled annals of the sea, the wreck of the brig *Polly* deserves a special place. There have been other ships, dismasted and reduced to helpless derelicts, that drifted aimlessly over endless leagues of ocean until, heavy with water, they slipped quietly beneath the waves. But few drifted as far and perhaps none drifted longer than the *Polly*. From the time she capsized until she was sighted near the west coast of Africa, the stricken brig floated nearly 2,000 miles and was adrift six months, to the day.

The *Polly* was never an impressive vessel. Compared with the larger trading ships that put into Boston Harbor in 1811, carrying silks and tea from far-off China, she was a seagoing workhorse. Eighty feet long and 130 tons burden, she was roughly built and rode the water like a heavy, clumsy bird. But Captain W. L. Cazneau was proud of her. She was bound for Santa Cruz with lumber and salt for the sugar plantations, and while she set no speed records she was husky and seaworthy.

On December 15, 1811, the *Polly* was four days out of Boston Harbor. Captain Cazneau, a powerful man with long experience at sea, stood spread-legged at the wheel, gazing out over the expanse of blue water. At the moment he felt contented, for he had conquered the two obstacles that had troubled him the most. First, he had cleared the dangerous sands and hidden shoals off Cape Cod—a treacherous neck of land where many ships had been wrecked, including three in one day in 1802. Second, he had managed to evade the British men-of-war that cruised the coast, raiding merchantmen and impressing their seamen. Now the *Polly* was in the Gulf Stream, where the going would be easier.

On board, in addition to Cazneau, were first mate Nathaniel Paddock, an Indian cook called Moho, deckhands Samuel Badger, Daniel Howe and a Swede named Johnson, and a stocky sailor whose name does not survive. There was also a passenger, J. S. Hunt, and an 11-year-old Negro girl who had been entrusted to his care.

Unfortunately, Captain Cazneau's contentment did not last. Five days later, on December 20, the *Polly* was suddenly overwhelmed by a storm that roared out of the southeast. Cazneau had noted the threatening clouds scudding overhead and had his men shorten sail before darkness. They had hardly begun when the storm struck with a savagery that surprised even the hard-bitten and experienced crew that manned the *Polly*. Howling winds whistled through the *Polly*'s rigging, ripping canvas and whirling it away in tattered fragments. As the crew tried to heave the vessel to, great waves battered the little brig mercilessly, tossing, wrenching, and twisting her. Blinding rain lashed the deck, and the wild gale bent her tall spruce masts like reeds in a summer breeze.

Captain Cazneau, fighting the wheel, watched one of the seamen inch his way out along the topsail yard in an attempt to reef the sail. But the savage wind clawed at the canvas and tore it to shreds before he could reach it. Then, under the relentless pounding of the ocean, the seams of the hull opened and water poured in until it was six feet deep. The stricken brig listed sharply to port, and Captain Cazneau sensed that the *Polly* was doomed.

Pitching and rolling in the mountainous waves, the gallant little brig battled the storm until midnight, when she suddenly trembled like a wounded animal and broached to. The next instant she capsized and lay like a dead whale on her side as the sea washed over her.

But the stoutness of the brig and the crew's seamanship were forces that the seas could not defeat. The captain, first mate Paddock, the four seamen and the cook managed to cling to the rigging, refusing to admit that the ship was dying—or that their own lives were as good as lost. Cazneau fought to keep his head above the swirling waters as he inched out onto one of the masts. Through the blinding spray he saw the others clinging to the shrouds, refusing to be washed away. To his amazement he saw that Samuel Badger even had an axe in his hand!

"Chop the rigging!" Cazneau screamed over the shrieking wind. "If the masts go, she may right herself!"

Desperately, Badger hacked away at the foremast until he was exhausted. Then Cazneau took over, fighting to keep his head above water as he flailed away. At last the foremast floated away from the capsized ship, and another seaman took the axe and started on the mainmast. Soon it, too, fell away. The sea, as if angered by this threat to its authority, hammered the capsized *Polly* with a giant wave. But the brig, relieved of its masts, defied the ocean and righted herself.

With hope suddenly renewed, the crew slashed with their knives at the tangled mass of spars and ropes until they drifted clean. Then they collapsed exhausted on the deck, letting the waves wash over them, not caring, knowing only that they were still afloat—and alive.

When daylight came it was still stormy, but the greatest violence of the sou'easter had passed. Searching the ravaged deck, Captain Cazneau discovered that the passenger, Mr. Hunt, had been swept overboard. The 11-year-old girl had somehow clung to the wreck, but the sea had battered her slim body so brutally that she died within a few hours. Captain Cazneau, mate Paddock, the four seamen, and Moho, the cook, had survived—and now rode a hulk that would drift endlessly with the currents and the winds into nowhere.

The prospect, Captain Cazneau thought, was far from cheerful, but at least they had no worries about food. There were a hundred barrels of salt pork and beef in the hold. There were also many casks of water. With any luck they would survive until some passing ship sighted the *Polly* and took them off.

It was a shock when the men discovered that all the water barrels had been smashed except for one 30-gallon cask that had been lashed to the quarterdeck. But they fished three barrels of salted meat from the hold and rolled them to the galley. Having no way to build a fire in the galley oven, they had to eat the salty stuff raw, but at least it was food—and they were thankful for it.

By the next morning the sea subsided and lay like a blue-green carpet beneath them. The sun, vaulting into the sky, promised a bright, mild day. Sluggishly, the *Polly* drifted out into the Atlantic, away from the Gulf Stream, her bow pointed in a southeasterly direction. She lay low in the water, with no masts or spars to mark her presence on the vastness of the ocean. She was too proud to sink —so she drifted, slowly and ponderously, to a destination the crew could only guess.

Twelve long days passed—all of them marked by a monotony that, Cazneau feared, might in the end drive them to insanity. The raw salted meat aggravated their thirst far beyond their capacity to satisfy it, for they were forced to ration their water to a quart a day per man. Within a short time their bodies, constantly exposed to the salt spray and the sun, became raw and blistered and developed festering sores that would not heal.

During the heat of the day, they took refuge from the

sun under a tattered canvas awning they rigged over the main hatch. But at all times one man remained on the afterdeck, scanning the wide world of water for a sail that might mean rescue.

On the 12th day Samuel Badger threw a piece of salt pork overboard with an oath. "Not fit for swine!" he growled. "If we only had some way to cook the stuff!"

Moho, the Indian cook, looked at Badger intently. A long lost art practiced by his ancestors stirred in his mind. Taking his knife from his belt, he stood up stiffly. "Me make fire," he announced laconically.

Captain Cazneau and the crew followed Moho out on deck. The Indian, paying no attention to the watching crew, split a pine spar with the axe, then gouged a sliver of wood from the oak rail of the ship. Carefully he cut two sticks from the inside cut of the oak, which had not been soaked by the sea. Then he set to work, grunting and sweating, trying to start a flame by friction heat. Eagerly, the crew gathered hemp and oakum from the beams of the ship for tinder—then waited breathlessly for the sight of a tiny flame.

It was no easy job. After a while most of the crew lost interest in the Indian's attempt to produce fire. "I heard they used to start fires that way," the stocky sailor said contemptuously, "but I ain't never believed it."

But Captain Cazneau, who had more confidence than the rest, watched Moho until at last the tinder began to smolder, and then a tiny flame set the oakum ablaze. Cazneau's shout of triumph brought the men racing back to the scene.

There was great excitement over the Indian's feat, and the flame was carefully transferred to the brick oven of the galley, where the men boiled the salted pork and beef. That night they enjoyed the biggest feast they had had since the storm. They stuffed themselves blissfully. They

had not yet discovered that the stern post of the *Polly* had
been staved in under water, and that the hundred barrels
of meat stored there had disappeared into the sea.

As the days wore on, the men acquired long, shaggy
beards that became encrusted with salt. Their bodies,
despite the meat they had consumed, grew gaunt and
emaciated, and their eyes became hollow black cavities.
Their clothing disintegrated into rags and the angry sores
on their bodies multiplied until they looked like lepers.

The precious cask of water lasted only 18 days. Rain
squalls, coming at infrequent intervals, added a little to
their water supply, but never enough to remove the threat
that they might all perish of thirst. Suffering with parched
throats and swelling tongues, they managed to reach the
40th day. The three barrels of meat they had originally
taken out of the hold were now empty, and Captain Cazneau sent Samuel Badger and Johnson into the hold of the
brig to float a few more barrels out into the hatch opening.

"At least," he said, "we have a hundred barrels of the
damned meat—so we won't starve!"

The two men lowered themselves into the flooded hold
and after some time reappeared, wet and bedraggled,
their eyes wild and unbelieving.

"The meat's gone!" Badger said. "The stern post is
smashed in, and all the cargo is gone except some
lumber."

Captain Cazneau's ruddy face paled. "We have nothing? No food at all?"

"Not a rotten thing," Badger said.

It was the final cruel blow. The short water supply was
bad enough, but there was always hope of rain. Now,
hopelessness seized the crew. They slumped to the deck
in gloomy silence, contemplating their fate. Captain Cazneau looked at them with concern and pity. He knew that
maintaining morale among the men was a vital thing—

that it could overcome obstacles and carry them through terrible hardships. But how could he keep up their morale now? How could he buoy their spirits? Was there, really, any reason for trying, now that their plight was so hopeless? Wasn't it better, perhaps, to stop fighting, to die peacefully and put an end to all this suffering?

Captain Cazneau couldn't stop these thoughts. He knew that the situation was even more alarming than some of the crew realized. With no food and very little water—and a blazing sun overhead that daily became worse—the *Polly* was continuing to drift in a southeasterly direction. She was caught in the Gulf Stream that skirts the coast of Africa and eventually enters the Gulf of Guinea. Her drift was taking her away from the trade routes to Europe and into the trackless spaces of the horse latitudes and the South Atlantic.

He sat on the hatchway coaming and looked at his men with fondness. They were good men, all of them— seafaring men who accepted the hardships of their calling and who battled for life even under the most impossible conditions. But there was a limit to what any man could endure, and the captain wondered if now, with all their food and most of their water gone, their limit had not been reached.

Ten more harrowing days crept by. Existing only on a small amount of water a day, and no food, the men quickly became walking skeletons. Cazneau felt as if a batch of fishhooks were stuck in his stomach, all pulling painfully in opposite directions. He watched Badger and Howe and Paddock wither before his eyes. The big Swede, Johnson, looked smaller to him.

During these ten days the men scanned the skies constantly for rain, but none fell. Once the weather grew rough, and they lay flat on the deck like miserable animals as the sea washed over them. Then the seas calmed and the sun returned, and with it the terrible heat that parched their throats and swelled their tongues until they could barely talk. Hours were spent dangling baitless hooks made of bent nails over the side of the *Polly*, in a futile effort to catch fish. Captain Cazneau even managed to inspire the heartsick men to carry some of the lumber out of the hold and build a crude shelter—a job that sapped their strength but at least gave them something to occupy their minds.

But the men had little real hope left. They watched one another almost calculatingly, wondering who would be the first to die. They were reduced to frail wretches whose skin was stretched tightly over protruding bones, and living had become almost unbearable.

The first death came on the 50th day after the storm. During the night the first mate, Paddock, quietly stopped breathing. The death surprised and shocked them, for as the old record states, "he was a man of robust constitution who had spent his life in fishing on the Grand Banks, was accustomed to endure privations, and appeared the most capable of standing the shocks of misfortune of any of the crew."

Quietly and with sad dignity, they slid Paddock's body into the sea. When the burial was over, Captain Cazneau talked to his remaining men. "We can die of starvation as Paddock did, or we can go mad," he told them bluntly. "The only thing to do is to keep busy. We must continue to take turns improving our shelter, we must fish no matter how hopeless, and we must work even though it exhausts us." And the crew, knowing the wisdom of what he said, fell to the tasks doggedly—though the shelter they erected was little help, and the fishing continued to prove unproductive.

On the 56th day, seamen Daniel Howe died. His passing brought a special kind of terror to the five survivors, for he died thrashing about in delirium and babbling incoherently. Quickly, wanting to get it over with, they dispatched his body to the sea, and the five who were left stared at each other, wondering.

Captain Cazneau was becoming more and more desperate. Not only did he want to go on living, but he felt a nagging responsibility for his crew—a feeling that he wasn't doing everything he could for them. He recognized that while food was important, water was vital—and now there wasn't a drop aboard. The sky was a glittering blue, with no prospect of rain. Not knowing what he hoped to find, he lowered himself into the dank hold of the ship and searched the slimy waters for whatever he could salvage. A few minutes later he bobbed up in the hatchway with an iron teakettle and a flintlock pistol.

These seemed to be objects of little use, yet Captain Cazneau took them to the makeshift shelter and sat there for several hours toying with them and thinking. What could he do with these? How could they be useful?

At last he had an idea. Fetching an iron pot from the galley, he turned the teakettle upside down on it. When the rims did not fit together, he took out his knife and began to whittle. After several hours of work he had managed to fashion a collar that permitted the pot and the kettle to be joined. Using pitch from the deck beams, he made the joint tight and waterproof. Then, knocking off the stock of the pistol, he used the long barrel as a tube, rammed it into the spout of the kettle and calked it soundly. The result was a crude instrument for distilling sea water.

The hollow faces of the seamen lighted up as they realized what the captain had done.

"By God, a still!" Badger exclaimed thickly. "You think she'll work?"

"It's got to work," Captain Cazneau said softly.

He was right about that. This was their last chance at survival. If it failed they would all be dead in a matter of days.

They carried the contrivance as tenderly as a baby to the brick oven. Captain Cazneau had wisely saved the flint and steel from the pistol, and they struck sparks from the flint to ignite shredded oakum in the oven. In a few minutes steam was hissing from the pistol barrel, and the crewmen poured cool salt water over the upturned spout of the teakettle to cause condensation. A rousing cheer went up from the five half-dead seamen as a trickle of water dropped from the pistol barrel into a tin cup.

Drop by drop the precious fluid trickled from the pistol barrel. They worked in shifts to produce the precious fluid, stoking the fire, lugging salt water, keeping the crude still operating night and day. Like robots they stayed at their monotonous task—and by their patient efforts they distilled enough sea water to give each man "four small wine glasses" a day.

Miraculously, with this invention, the situation began to improve aboard the *Polly*.

One of the seamen seemingly achieved the impossible when he looped a bowline over the tail of a shark and hoisted the creature aboard, and this supplied the crew with food for several days. Also, warm-water barnacles began clinging to the sodden hull of the *Polly*, and these the seamen scraped off—and ate raw. Cooking them would have interfered with the still. Such food and drink kept them alive, but it wasn't to give them stamina—and as the days became weeks, their strength ebbed, and the pain of starvation gnawed at them incessantly.

On March 15—having been adrift for three months —Moho, the Indian cook, died quietly and with dignity. The captain's log reported, "Moho gave up the ghost . . . though with much less distress than the others and in full exercise of his reason." The survivors—Captain Cazneau, Badger, Johnson, and the chunky sailor—huddled over the body, their minds plagued by strange thoughts. Badger glanced up at Cazneau, his brow furrowed.

"We're starving," he said simply, as he looked at the cook's body.

Captain Cazneau shook his head. "We won't have cannibalism aboard the ship," he said.

Badger scowled. "You'd rather feed the fishes?"

"There'll be no cannibalism," Cazneau insisted.

Finally, they compromised. Before delivering Moho's body to the sea, they cut off one of his legs. Slicing the flesh into strips, they used the pieces for shark bait. The strategy worked, for they caught a huge shark that supplied them with food for a full week.

Once again searching the hold for usable material, Captain Cazneau located another pistol. He used the barrel to lengthen the spout of the teakettle and thus gained more cooling surface for condensation. The new arrangement increased their production of fresh water to "eight junk bottles full" each 24 hours. To supplement their supply, they built wooden gutters to catch rain and deposit it in empty casks.

April brought spring weather to the rest of the world, but to the four survivors on the *Polly* it brought only the same endless, tropical days they had already endured so long. It also brought another death, despite their improved conditions. Johnson, the huge Swede, who had faded away to a gaunt and feeble 100 pounds, slipped into delirium and died. Aboard the *Polly* now were only three men—Captain Cazneau, Badger, and the chunky sailor.

One morning toward the end of April, the three men awoke to find the derelict becalmed in the middle of an endless carpet of seaweed. Captain Cazneau looked at the frightened expressions on the faces of his two companions and shuddered inwardly.

"The Sargasso!" Badger choked.

Captain Cazneau grunted dispiritedly. It seemed that the *Polly* had now truly doomed herself. She had drifted into the fabled area of the Atlantic known as the Sargasso Sea, which lies still and dead between the Azores and the Antilles. The area was dreaded by all seamen. Here was nothing but great expanses of stagnant ocean, moving slowly in circles—a place where tangled patches of red and brown and green seaweed tugged and trailed at the hulls of ships until they throttled all motion. It was well-known that many ships caught in the Sargasso Sea had not been able to extricate themselves, and had rotted until the ship fell apart and sank. The *Polly* could expect nothing better. Without masts or sails to push her through the leathery kelp, she would finally come to rest in this calm wasteland and slowly die.

"After four months adrift," Badger said sadly, "you would think the Good Lord could spare us this."

"So we die in the Sargasso—what difference?" the sailor said, shrugging his thin shoulders. "A lot of good sailors have died here before us."

Captain Cazneau's face flushed with anger. "You're giving up!" he snapped impatiently. "We've come this far and lived—and we can go on living. We have pure water now and maybe—" he glanced over the rail at the clinging mass of seaweed "—maybe, by the grace of God, the Sargasso Sea will help us instead of destroying us!"

The two men looked askance at the captain. Perhaps he was slipping. They had watched it happen to the others, and now it was happening to him. The loss of reason, the insane chatter, the incoherent babbling, then the delirious cries, and finally, death.

They watched curiously as Captain Cazneau lowered a bucket over the rail of the ship and filled it with the stinking water of the Sargasso. Hauling the bucket up and setting it on the deck, he pulled out a tangled mass of kelp. A triumphant shout ripped from his throat.

"There, dammit! Look at that, will you? Crabs! Crabs by the hundreds!"

The crew stared with disbelief. Gaudy colored crabs clung tenaciously to the seaweed. In the dreaded doldrums of the Sargasso Sea there seemed to be enough food for an army!

Heartened by this, the three skeletons on the derelict lowered bucket after bucket overboard, eating the crabs raw as they caught them. They gorged themselves on the succulent crustaceans until their stomachs screamed in pain. Then they threw lines over the side with bent nail fishhooks, and caught small multicolored fish that they cleaned, rubbed with salt taken from the still, and dried in the sun for future use.

Time dragged by. Days in the strange ocean wilderness were bright and hot. The *Polly* barely moved in the clutch of matted seaweed, lying low and motionless as if she had decided there was no escape from her mushy prison. The air was still and fetid, and the three men lived like unthinking automatons, working and fishing at Captain Cazneau's orders, but almost insensible to their surroundings.

Sometime during the month of May the chunky sailor, despite the fact that food was more plentiful, weakened and died. On the sluggish derelict there now remained only Captain Cazneau and seaman Samuel Badger.

Still striving to maintain their sanity, the two survivors did useless work. With a bundle of shingles discovered in the hold and a keg of nails found in a corner of the fo'c'sle, they continued to work on their rough shelter, "which by constant improvement had become much more commodious." Actually, with only two of them left, there was no need for more room. But the work kept them busy and not brooding—and this was important.

Then, one day, the two men noticed that the tangle of weeds was parting and that the *Polly* was about to leave the Sargasso Sea and move again into the open Atlantic. They greeted the event with mixed feelings.

"We're free of the Sargasso!" Badger exulted, but he noticed a frown on Captain Cazneau's face.

"We're free of the food too," the captain said. "I don't know whether it's better to be trapped in the Sargasso where we can eat, or freed to drift without food."

"We have some dried fish," Badger said hopefully.

The captain nodded. In any case, there was little they could do about it. Without guidance or destination the *Polly* was moving in some aimless pattern. Cazneau noted with hope that she was now drifting toward the waters where Yankee ships, taking advantage of trade wind routes, slanted far over to the African coast. She was also in the path of East Indiamen who plied the waters between English ports and the Cape of Good Hope. They had reached waters where rescue was at least a possibility.

But the low silhouette of the derelict worked against them. Through most of May and well into the month of June, Captain Cazneau frequently spotted white sails against the blue skyline, but all of them sailed on without sighting the *Polly*. By the 19th of June they had drifted into the vicinity of the Canary Islands—almost 2,000 miles from the point where the *Polly* had capsized. Her average rate of drift had been about 300 miles a month, or ten miles a day. Six harrowing months had passed, and of the original crew of seven, only the two remained alive.

Then June 20 arrived. It dawned like any other day, a

bright, brittle day that bore no more promise than any other day. Captain Cazneau was standing near the hatchway when the unbelievable sight appeared. His heart leaped agonizingly in his chest as he pointed a tremulous finger out over the sparkling sea.

"Ships!" he croaked. "Three ships! British, they are!"

Badger was so overwhelmed with excitement that he leaped up and down like a demented child as he saw the three ships slanting toward them. Finally he exhausted himself and had to lean against the rail to catch his breath. Captain Cazneau sat wearily down upon the hatch coaming, wanting only to rest now that the ordeal was approaching its end.

The three ships were a beautiful sight—tall and graceful, and smartly handled, each flying the red ensign of Great Britain from her spanker gaff. When Captain Featherstone of the *Fame* called his greeting through his brass trumpet, Cazneau found that an aching lump in his throat made it impossible for him to answer. He buried his face in his hands and allowed tears of thanksgiving to flow between his fingers. Badger, exhausted from his joyous exertions, collapsed on the deck.

Presently a jolly boat was lowered from the davits of the *Fame*, and in a few minutes Captain W. L. Cazneau and seaman Samuel Badger were transferred to the British ship. Captain Featherstone, whose ship was homeward bound from Rio de Janeiro, fed and clothed the ragged castaways and gave them the best of care.

That night the captains of the three ships that had been traveling in company dined together on the *Fame* and listened with open-mouthed amazement at the tale told by the rescued men. A few days later Cazneau and Badger were transferred to the American brig *Dromo*, which carried the *Polly*'s survivors back to Boston. At home they were greeted as heroes, for the *Polly* had long ago been given up as "missing with all hands."

The story of how the intrepid little brig had survived six months of drifting—and how two seamen had survived with her—became one of the classic waterfront yarns of the time. In due time Captain Cazneau and Badger returned to the sea—as most dedicated seamen do—this time aboard an American privateer whose job it was, ironically, to prey upon British shipping. The War of 1812 between Britain and America had begun on June 18, 1812—two days before Cazneau and Badger were rescued by the British ship *Fame*.

The *Polly* was never sighted again. When Cazneau and Badger were rescued, she was drifting at latitude 28° North and longitude 130° West—not far from the west coast of Africa. By any manner of reckoning, her ultimate fate should have been a watery grave. But after stubbornly refusing to sink for over six months, it is entirely possible that she never sank at all—but continued her weird journey until she was washed up on some deserted African shore, to rot away in the dryness of the sun.

3

The Ghastly Wreck of
the *Medusa* (1816)

O N the afternoon of June 17, 1816, the forty-
four gun French frigate *Medusa*, crowded to the gunwales with 400 passengers, slid gracefully out of the roadsteads of Rochefort, France, into the open sea. In her
wake were three other ships of the flotilla—the corvette
Echo, the brig *Argus*, and the flute *La Loire*—all destined
for the French West African colony of Senegal.

Even in 1816 the trip to Senegal was considered
neither difficult nor dangerous. Yet, because of an incom-
petent captain, who spent more time attending to the
desires of his mistress than to the needs of his ship, the
voyage of the *Medusa* was fated to end in spectacular
disaster. To this day the wreck of the *Medusa* and its
terrifying aftermath stand as one of the most ghastly sea
tragedies in history. While many shipwrecks have inspired heroism, self-sacrifice, and discipline, the demise
of the *Medusa* resulted only in savagery, mass murder,

and cannibalism—with 138 people perishing in a useless
bloodbath that has no counterpart in the history of the sea.

M. Alexandre Correard, a naturalist, stood at the taffrail
of the *Medusa* studying the assortment of passengers
aboard the ship. There were career soldiers and sailors,
meticulous clerks and engineers, hardened criminals and
dedicated students, women of breeding and degraded
prostitutes—a diverse combination of riffraff and respec-
tability that, Correard thought, sprang directly from the
political turbulence that had made this voyage necessary.
The remains of Napoleon Bonaparte's army lay scattered
and rotting on the field at Waterloo, Napoleon himself
was in exile at Elba, and the monarchy had been restored
to France—in the personage of fat, inept, and ruthless
Louis XVIII. The victorious British, in a moment of rare
generosity, had returned to France, among other possessions, the colony of Senegal, and the *Medusa* was carrying
the newly appointed governor of the colony as well as
men of various talents who would build the possession to
a status commensurate with the importance of France as a
nation. In addition to civilian passengers, there were 252
soldiers, mainly drafted from three Negro regiments
under French officers, and the crew.

Correard turned to his friend, surgeon Jean Baptiste
Henri Savigny, with a wry smile.

"A pompous devil, isn't he?" he said, motioning to
Julien Schmaltz, the new French Governor of Senegal,
who stood on the afterdeck brushing imaginary pieces of
lint from his lace and velvet sleeves.

"An elegant relic of pre-Revolutionary days," agreed
Savigny. "And have a look at de Chaumareys!"

Hugues Deroys, Vicomte de Chaumareys, had been
appointed captain of the frigate *Medusa*, not because of
his experience but because he was a personal friend of

Louis XVIII. He knew little of ships, less of the sea, and nothing at all of West African waters. Once, when the infamous Louis XVI graced the throne, de Chaumareys had spent some time in the French Navy—but not enough to learn much, if indeed he had wanted to. When the French peasants rose in revolt against the throne in 1789, de Chaumareys immediately sensed that his aristocratic connections put him in line for a trip to the guillotine, so he decided to take a trip to England instead. He did not return until the end of the Napoleonic Wars in 1815, and when he did, he lost no time ingratiating himself with Louis XVIII. The King rewarded his loyalty by naming him captain of the *Medusa*, bound for Senegal to rescue what remained of France's colonial glory. Basking in the glow of his new command, de Chaumareys, with a heavily painted prostitute on his arm, stood near Governor Schmaltz's family.

"I dare say," said Correard, "that de Chaumareys will be more interested in his *fille de joie* than his ship."

"Ah, that he will! He was something of a scoundrel before the Revolution, you know. And as a seaman—well, he's less than adequate. He knows nothing of the waters we'll be plying, and that makes for a dangerous situation."

How dangerous even Correard and Savigny could not have guessed—for the voyage of the *Medusa* seemed doomed from the beginning. Captain de Chaumareys started out by ignoring his maps, since he did not know how to read them anyway, and by refusing in his arrogance to accept advice from his more experienced officers. A combination of slack winds and de Chaumarey's bungling wasted eight days before the flotilla arrived at Cape Finisterre. After leaving this port, the *Medusa* picked up a good wind and, being the fastest ship of the four, soon left her protective escort behind. Unwilling to listen to his better-informed officers, de Chaumareys guided his ship by luck and the grace of God—and promptly sailed a hundred miles off course before reaching Tenerife, the largest of the Canary Islands and the last port of call before Senegal.

One indication of de Chaumareys' unconcern for those whose lives rested in his hands occurred as the *Medusa* was making good time with a favorable breeze billowing her sails. One of the cabin boys fell overboard, and when a passenger hurried to tell the captain about the accident, he simply spread his hands in a helpless gesture.

"I'm sorry, but I can't slow the ship down to pick up the boy," he said.

When several passengers pleaded with him, he reluctantly lowered a boat, and three seamen went in search of the boy. But they conducted only a perfunctory search, afraid that de Chaumareys might abandon them too, and returned to the ship. The boy was never found.

"We did our best," said de Chaumareys righteously.

Between Tenerife and Senegal, de Chaumareys knew he would have to skirt a treacherous barrier of shallow waters and sunken rocks known as the Arguin Reef, but apparently this didn't alarm him unduly. When a passenger who once had been shipwrecked on the reef offered advice, de Chaumareys brushed him off and turned instead to a suave individual named M. Richefort, a member of the Cape Verde Philanthropical Society. Richefort knew as little about seamanship as de Chaumareys but pretended to be knowledgeable. Because de Chaumareys found cabin life with his mistress more inviting than guiding his ship, he virtually relinquished command of the ship to Richefort—and this reliance on a second inept man proved to be the coup de grace of the *Medusa*.

Under Richefort's command, the *Medusa* set a perilous

course closer to the African shore than any navigator would have recommended. Puzzled by the strange actions of the flagship, the other three ships in the flotilla refused to follow, traveling around the reef by the mapped route, far out of sight of the *Medusa*.

On the first of July the *Medusa* crossed the Tropic of Cancer. To de Chaumareys, who emerged from his cabin with his mistress on his arm and his belly full of wine, this called for a celebration. He ordered those who could play the fiddle to strike up some music, and before long the passengers were dancing on the deck, most of them unaware of approaching danger. During the height of the merriment one of the ship's officers approached de Chaumareys.

"My reckoning is that we're over the Arguin Bank," he reported.

The captain waved him away. "Don't worry, my lad. There are a hundred fathoms of water under our keel."

But de Chaumareys was wrong. At that very moment the ship was entering shallow water where a labyrinth of reefs and shoals jutted far out from the African coast. Minutes later the ship shuddered violently and came to an abrupt halt, scattering the dancing passengers across the deck. The ship's officer had reckoned correctly. The *Medusa* had run aground on the Arguin Bank in sixteen feet of water and lay about sixty miles off the coast of Africa.

Although the shock to the passengers was great, the *Medusa* had actually grounded lightly. Damage was minimal, and the ship was in no immediate danger of going down. There were six seaworthy boats available, enough to carry 250 of the 400 persons aboard to land and return for the rest. A seasoned commander would have put a rescue plan into operation at once, but de Chaumareys and the inexperienced Richefort had no presence of mind. They were confused and indecisive, and instead of calm discipline in the face of adversity, pandemonium resulted. Frightened sailors stormed the deck demanding action and had to be driven below by the swords of their officers. Passengers wept and prayed, and one vengeful group tried to find Richefort and throw him to the sharks—but the culprit hid in a remote part of the ship. Captain de Chaumareys found himself threatened by angry passengers and was at a loss to correct the deteriorating situation.

"If we lighten her by throwing over the stocks of flour and a few of the guns," said one seaman, "she might float free."

"We will need the provisions in Senegal," objected de Chaumareys. "There must be another way."

"We can try kedging," suggested Correard softly.

This was a new word to de Chaumareys, but his crew knew what was meant. With axes they cut away the topmasts, then dropped the kedge anchor in an attempt to pull the *Medusa* free. But the ship only drifted farther onto the reef and then contentedly embedded herself even more deeply.

"We might sit here for a long time," said one of the officers, "but our best course is to get the people off the ship and into the boats. If a strong wind comes up, it might tear the ship to pieces."

"This is a seaworthy craft!" snapped de Chaumareys stubbornly. "No wind is going to destroy the *Medusa*."

Again de Chaumareys was wrong. That night, as she lay helpless, a stiff gale rose, and waves buffeted the stricken ship. It was the beginning of the end. All at once the great rudder swung off its gudgeons, sweeping back and forth as it hammered and splintered the stern. Water leaked into some of the cabins, and the hull planks began to part. It was finally obvious, even to de Chaumareys, that the

Medusa was doomed and would have to be abandoned.

For the rest of the long night much talk ensued, but little action. Without firm leadership from de Chaumareys, the passengers, crew, and soldiers argued about who should be taken first in the six boats. It was feared that if the boats set out for shore with 250 of the 400 people aboard, they would never again return to the ship. With suspicion and distrust running rampant and no one strong enough to take charge, the situation worsened rapidly. The crew became mutinous, the ship's officers grumbled about de Chaumareys, and the passengers grew restless and more fearful. An uneasy night passed.

In the morning Governor Julien Schmaltz, puffing proudly with his own brilliancy, suggested a solution to the problem.

"I suggest that a large raft be built from the ship's topmasts, yards, and booms," he said. "The six boats will then tow the raft behind them. Thus, we will all escape the *Medusa* at one time."

It sounded like a good idea, and all that day the sailors labored to join the various pieces of wood together with nails and rope. The raft was triangular in shape, with the pointed end designed to cut the water as it was towed. Boards were nailed over this frame, but when the job was finished, the raft was not seaworthy. It was a hasty, ill-conceived job, and few wanted to risk their lives on it. As a result there was a stampede and much confusion as passengers, crew, and soldiers vied for the safest positions in the six boats.

Savigny later described the raft in the following manner: "The raft, from one extremity to the other, was at least twenty metres [about 66 feet] in length, and about seven metres [approximately 22 feet] in breadth; this length might induce one to think that at first sight it was able to carry 200 men, but we soon had cruel proofs of its weakness."

The raft was, in fact, so badly constructed that there was barely room for 15 people to stretch out comfortably. Yet this rickety construction was forced to carry 147 people (soldiers, officers, sailors, and passengers, including one intrepid woman) as well as six kegs of wine, two casks of water, and several casks of flour. To make matters worse, some of the sailors and soldiers were drunk and were hardly fit companions in a time of distress.

When the raft was fully loaded, the miserable castaways stood almost waist-deep in water. Those in the boats, however, were in much better circumstances. And, of course, Captain de Chaumareys, his mistress, and Governor Schmaltz and his family made certain that they had the best accommodations and provisions possible. In fact, the aristocratic Schmaltz had insisted that he be lowered over the rail in his armchair.

Correard and Savigny volunteered for the raft, hoping to be of help to some of the miserable wretches assigned there. Seventeen men, unable to get into the crowded boats and looking askance at the raft, decided to stay on the *Medusa* and gamble that they would be sighted and rescued.

At last the raft and the boats were loaded and ready to depart. Someone in the Governor's boat hoisted the white flag of the Bourbon monarchy as the boats headed for shore sixty miles away, and the lines from the six boats to the raft tightened. It looked as if, despite de Chaumareys' incompetence, most of the people would survive the wreck of the *Medusa*.

It was not to be. Within two leagues of the *Medusa* those in the boats began to have doubts that their small crafts, badly rigged and already shipping water, would make shore if they were required to tow the cumbersome raft. One by one they dropped the towropes until only Governor Schmaltz's boat remained tied to the raft. Suddenly the frightened people on the raft heard a voice carry over the quiet of the sea.

"Let us abandon them."

Immediately an officer in the Governor's boat cut the towrope, and the raft was left wallowing in the sea as the boats pulled away.

Correard looked at Savigny and shook his head in disbelief. Then his eyes scanned the 147 people huddled together on the raft, in imminent danger of slipping off into the ocean or falling through the planking of the raft. Except for a handful of officers with some conception of discipline, there was only a crew of rough and half-drunken sailors who already teetered on the edge of mutiny.

The wind was off the sea, and the desperate people on the raft watched as the sails on the six departing boats caught the breeze and headed for shore. Soon they became only specks in the distance, and the raft, with no sail, creaked and groaned in the water—a helpless derelict.

Correard, Savigny, and a midshipman named Caudin were the three who seemed to possess the most qualities of leadership. Correard finally gathered together a piece of canvas that had been thrown to them from the *Medusa* and erected a makeshift mast, using a board stripped from the raft and the rope from Governor Schmaltz's boat. Then, having done all they could, the people huddled together and prayed.

From the very first, the six kegs of wine threatened trouble. The drunken sailors and soldiers grumbled and menaced the few officers who guarded and refused to open the kegs. Toward evening the officers passed a small portion of wine to each person aboard, but it was only enough to whet the appetites of the crewmen.

Then darkness fell—the first long night to be spent upon the rickety raft.

The night was disastrous. The wind rose as darkness descended, and waves battered the unsteady raft. The middle of the raft was the safest and strongest part, and the frightened people all tried to crowd to the center. Those who could not make it, were swept from the pitching raft and lost in the blackness of the sea. Others slipped through the planking and were ground to death as the sea manipulated the unstable raft like an accordion. When dawn broke and the nightmare was over, Correard and Savigny counted the survivors.

The count was 127. Twenty men were missing.

During the long day the raft drifted aimlessly, the mast catching very little breeze. The survivors became half-crazed with thirst. The flour casks had been thrown overboard to lighten the weight on the raft, and only water and wine remained. The officers, armed with sabers, maintained their guard over the kegs. They rationed the water carefully but wisely refused to open the wine casks again. Several men, unable to cope with the extreme conditions of thirst, hunger, and constant danger, leaped into the sea to end their misery.

And the second night came—and with it a violent storm.

Savigny later wrote: "If the preceding night had been terrible, this was still more horrible. Mountains of water covered us every moment; very happily we had the wind behind us, and the fury of the waves was a little checked by the rapidity of the progress with which we drove towards land. From the violence of the sea the men passed rapidly from the back to the front of the raft. We tried to keep in the centre, the most solid part of the raft, and those who could not get there almost perished. Before and behind, the waves dashed with fury, and carried off the men in spite of their resistance."

All through the night the raft pitched wildly in the churning waters. And as if the storm was not enough, the sailors became more and more unruly.

"We're all going to die, by God!" they screamed at their officers. "Give us the wine!"

The officers, with Correard, Savigny, and most of the passengers, crowded around the wine kegs in the middle of the raft, fearing that if the desperate sailors reached it, there would be greater trouble. But they were heavily outnumbered, and finally a group of sailors reached a wine keg, dragged it away from the center of the raft, punched a hole in it, and began to drink from tin cups they had salvaged from the *Medusa*. The officers, rather than do battle on the pitching raft, decided to let them have the keg. But they vowed they would not let another one be stolen.

Within an hour many of the sailors and soldiers were drunk and beyond reason. Their minds crazed with fear and alcohol, some of them decided to murder the officers and then cut the raft apart in an orgy of suicide.

One burly sailor, who seemed to act as a leader, shouted drunkenly, "Get rid of the officers! There's no room on the raft for all, and the officers must go!"

The words fired the maddened minds of the mutineers. One grabbed a boarding axe and began to cut away at the ropes that bound the raft together. The burly sailor advanced threateningly toward the officers with a similar axe in his hand. An officer stepped forward, ran him through with a saber, and the fight was on.

Grabbing weapons, Correard, Savigny, Caudin, and some of the passengers, who wished to see the raft spared, joined the battle. The officers and passengers were on

one side, the sailors and soldiers on the other. The officers
had the best weapons; the passengers were badly armed.
Manpower was on the side of the mutineers.

In the black of the night the fighting raged. The sailor
who was cutting the raft's bindings was killed and thrown
into the sea. Others fell before the sabers of the officers;
many fell through the shifting planks of the raft and were
either drowned or mangled.

One berserk sailor managed to reach the makeshift
mast in the center of the raft and hacked it down. The mast
fell heavily on one of the officers, breaking his leg. Two
soldiers scooped him up and threw him into the boiling
sea, but several officers fished him out and lay him on the
raft.

Finally the main body of the mutineers was beaten
back by the superior swordsmanship of the officers, but
the officer with the broken leg was dragged away as a
hostage.

"Give us the wine and get rid of some of the useless
passengers," cried one of the mutineers, "or we'll cut out
this officer's eyes with a penknife!"

The hideous threat sickened Correard.

"We have no alternative," he said to a nearby officer.
"We have to charge them."

The officer nodded. Sabers drawn, the officers formed a
stout line, then rushed forward. The battle was ferocious.
On the madly bucking raft, the men slashed at each other
savagely. Blood stained the deck of the raft, and many of
the mutineers were shoved into the turbulent waters.

Correard distinguished himself during the battle.
Fighting with a saber, which was an unfamiliar weapon to
him, he slashed right and left until the mutineers feared
to come near him. It was during this wild melee that one
mutineer grabbed the lone woman and threw her overboard. Leaving the battle, Correard tied a rope around his

waist and dove in after her. In a tremendous struggle against the tempestuous sea, he managed to get her back to the raft, where he propped her against some dead bodies near the wine kegs, and then rejoined the fighting officers.

The first gray streaks of dawn were visible before the bloody combat ended. The storm had quieted and the raft, floating level now, was slippery with blood and pieces of human flesh. Dead bodies were everywhere, and the two groups of antagonists sat apart from each other, too exhausted to continue the fight. In addition to three men who had thrown themselves overboard during the day, 57 had died in the carnage during the night, leaving only 67 aboard the raft. Many of these survivors were wounded. Only one keg of wine had survived the storm and the battle; the rest had gone into the sea. And since both sides were too tired to fight, an uneasy peace prevailed.

A saffron sun rose in the sky, and the day became hot and sultry. The exhausted men, now tortured anew by the heat, sat as if in a stupor. Many became delirious and were beset with delusions and fantasies. For awhile, Correard imagined he was traveling through lovely country somewhere in Italy. Others babbled about food, as hunger gnawed at their innards; some believed they were about to dine elaborately in a Paris cafe. And while the fantasies of starvation gripped them, they tried to get sustenance by chewing on their shoulder belts and the sweatbands of hats. One sailor even attempted to eat excrement but was unable to do so.

Then the inevitable happened. The mutineers suddenly threw themselves upon the dead bodies and began to hack pieces from them with knives. Near starvation, they ate the human flesh raw. The officers and passengers looked on, horrified, and refused to eat the loathsome food.

By afternoon the intense heat of the sun had increased the thirst and hunger of the 67 still on the raft. A small school of flying fish swept under the raft at one point, and some of these were caught and eaten; but there were not enough to relieve the starving men. Eventually, even the officers and passengers were forced to eat some of the human flesh, which they first dried in the sun to "render it less disgusting."

That night, as the helpless band struggled upon the floundering raft, twelve more slid into the sea and died.

There were now 55 survivors on the raft.

Another day passed, a long, wearisome and hopeless day. The men scanned the horizon, hoping to see the sails of a ship coming toward them. Again they dreamed of dining in luxurious places, and again they hacked at the bodies of the dead and tore at the human flesh in the manner of savage dogs.

But the ghoulish food had only one effect on some of the men, it increased their belligerency. By nightfall a group of the sailors again became mutinous, hatching a plot to throw everyone into the sea except their own small group. Both sides fought desperately—hideous wraiths, covered with blood, battling under a pale moon. It was a war of attrition, with each man trying to kill as many of his opponents as possible on the theory that the fewer left on the raft, the better the chance of survival.

When dawn came again the number on the raft had been reduced to 30.

The fifth day and night passed peacefully, the utter exhaustion of the survivors making it impossible for them to do battle. The wounded were in agony as the salt water washed across their open battle sores. The next day—the sixth at sea—saw more trouble. Two sailors attempted to rush the remaining wine keg, and the officers picked them up bodily and tossed them into the sea. A young boy also died of wounds suffered during the earlier battles, leaving 27 on the raft.

Now a terrible decision had to be made. Of the 27 survivors, 12 were obviously dying, including the woman passenger. There was practically no food, and the lone keg of wine was the only thing to sustain them. Correard, Savigny, and the officers huddled in a group, talking in soft whispers.

"It's a frightful thing to contemplate," Correard said, "but we do not have food, and the wine will not sustain 27 people."

"The twelve weakest might live long enough to de-plete our supply of wine, but it will not save their lives," said one of the officers.

"There is no point in wasting our meager supply on those who will die anyway," reasoned Savigny.

There was a long consultation. "We have no choice," said Correard finally. "We must throw into the sea the twelve weakest among us, so that the rest can live."

Four stalwart sailors who had fought on the officers' side during the battles were selected to perform the grue-some task of execution. While the officers knelt in prayer, the sailors threw twelve people into the waters, including the woman. The agonized cries of those being sacrificed grated harshly on the survivors' ears, as they implored God to forgive them for the decision they had made.

When the macabre task was finished, Correard ad-dressed the remaining 15 on the raft.

"In our own self-interest," he said, "we must make peace. Only that way do we have a chance to survive."

All agreed, and to make sure there would be no further fighting, the 15 survivors threw away their weapons with the exception of one knife and sat down on the raft to await their rescue or their end.

It was the beginning of a long period of torment. The derelict raft continued to drift aimlessly. Thirst and hunger tortured the survivors, and they became emaciated and stupified by lack of food and drink. Their skins turned black under the merciless heat of the sun, their lips became parched and dry, their tongues lolled from half-open mouths. Saltwater sores appeared on their bodies, and most of them lay on the raft in excruciating agony. Reason left them.

A week went by, then two. The men could no longer stand but lay on the sea-washed raft resignedly awaiting death. One officer found thirty cloves of garlic in a small bag that had been miraculously overlooked by all of them, and the men clawed each other like beasts for this morsel of food. Another man found two phials of fluid for cleaning teeth, and this was shared and consumed. They even chewed pieces of pewter to keep their mouths moist. But nothing worked. They began to feel that those who had died quickly in the bloody battles had been the fortunate ones.

From time to time they were tortured by false hopes. One day Correard looked up at the mast that had again been raised and saw a white butterfly fluttering around it. Some of the other men noticed it at the same time.

"Land must be near!" Correard croaked. He could barely utter the words.

The men peered into the distance—an endless void of water and blue sky and nothing else.

"Where it came from I don't know," said one discouraged officer. "There is no land."

Sharks, which had followed the raft for days, nosed closer. An officer looked at them.

"I think I'll give them what they want," he said. "There is no hope, and the sharks will finish me off handily."

He started toward the edge of the raft, determined to throw himself into the sea, but was dragged back. He collapsed on the deck again and cried softly.

On the 17th day adrift help finally came. The brig *Argus*, one of the original ships in the flotilla that had left France, had reached Senegal and had been dispatched to find out what had happened to the *Medusa*, and now it bore down on them, white sails sparkling in the sunlight. The bearded, emaciated men on the raft were almost too weak to wave to the ship, and they crawled to the edge of the raft as the ship neared, whimpering in pain and crying like lost children.

The wretched band of survivors was transferred to the *Argus*, which immediately set sail for Senegal. Six more of the men died in Senegal, leaving only nine survivors, including Correard and Savigny, from the raft-load of 147.

It was not until seven days after those on the raft had reached safety that Governor Schmaltz sent a ship out to the stricken *Medusa* to determine if any of the 17 who had remained aboard still lived. And it was Correard who had to persuade Governor Schmaltz to undertake the rescue.

"I presume," the governor said condescendingly, "that we ought to send a ship out. After all, there is aboard some five thousand pounds of specie that would be worth having."

"And seventeen men aboard, too!" snapped Correard.

"Ah, yes." The Governor looked perturbed. "Although I doubt that more than three of them could have survived."

A ship was dispatched, but it was so badly equipped for the task of rescue that it had to return to port. It was not until 52 days after the *Medusa* had been abandoned that a ship actually reached the wreck on the reef.

The Governor was right. There were only three survivors. They were taken from the ship, but none lived
very long. Two died in Senegal, and the third was mur-
dered, possibly because he knew too much about the
desertion of the *Medusa* by Captain de Chaumareys and
Governor Schmaltz and was determined to speak out.

At great risk to themselves, because of their decision to
throw 12 people off the raft, Correard and Savigny were
nevertheless determined to place the blame for the wreck
of the *Medusa* where it belonged. They returned to
France and, several months later, published a full account
of the *Medusa*'s tragic story. Correard and Savigny were
publicly condemned for their hard decision to destroy
12 people and for a long time they were ostracized.

But the telling of the story had one beneficial result; it
so aroused the ire of the public that the French Government recalled both de Chaumareys and Governor
Schmaltz to France in disgrace. The *Medusa* saga was
complete—and duly recorded as the most horrible, and
most undisciplined, shipwreck in maritime history.

4

Demise of the
William Brown (1841)

I⊤ had been a perilous journey from the beginning. Out of Liverpool, England, and bound for Philadelphia, the American square-rigged sailing vessel *William Brown* had encountered nothing but storms and heavy fog for five weeks. Now, moving under shortened sail, she was entering a highly dangerous area—a field of massive icebergs.

Seaman Alexander William Holmes stood braced on the foredeck, staring into the soupy thickness of the fog. Captain George Harris came alongside.

"You can feel the cold breath of 'em, can't you?" he said, his lips tight.

"Aye!" Holmes nodded. "And I'd feel a lot better if I could also see 'em!"

That, of course, was the problem. The impenetrable fog had reduced visibility to the point where the *William Brown* traveled in constant danger. The fact that she could strike an iceberg before anyone could mount an alarm was a fearful threat, and that threat became a reality minutes after the exchange of conversation between Captain Harris and Holmes when a mountain of ice towered suddenly before them. It was as if the fog had momentarily lifted and opened a pathway to doom.

"Iceberg—starboard side!" Holmes shouted, but it was too late. There was a sickening crunch, and the *William Brown* lurched crazily, then listed hard to port. Holmes went sprawling across the deck, crashing against the portside rail. Clinging to the rail he staggered to his feet, and a cold feeling that was not caused by the breath of the iceberg washed over him. His sea experience had already told him the shocking truth.

The *William Brown* was sinking . . .

It was March 13, 1841, when the 560-ton *William Brown* departed from Liverpool and slipped down the Mersey River toward the open sea. She carried a full complement of cargo, along with 65 Scottish and Irish immigrants who huddled in the cramped quarters of the steerage. They were hardy folk willing to gamble on an Atlantic crossing at a less-than-ideal time of the year to seek a better way of life in America, and the ship's crew of 17 admired them for their courage.

The *William Brown* was under the command of Captain George Harris, first mate Francis Rhodes, and second mate Walter Parker. All were experienced seamen who knew well the vicissitudes of the sea and, despite the fact that sea disasters were not uncommon in those days, there was every expectation that the *William Brown* would accomplish the crossing safely.

But difficulties plagued the ship almost from the moment it reached the mouth of the river and entered the choppy waters of the Atlantic. Few vessels before or since have made crossings under more adverse conditions

The bad weather never let up. Rain, sleet, and wind storms seemed to compete with one another in attempts to destroy the *William Brown*. The ship's sails were ripped by savage winds time after time, and the crew was kept busy repairing and replacing yards of canvas. The ship itself creaked and groaned as great waves washed over her decks, and sometimes she shuddered so violently that the passengers were convinced that the ship was on the point of breaking in two.

For 23 days there was no relief from the frenzied storms. One followed on the heels of another like soldiers marching in a parade. As she battled the elements, the *William Brown* rolled and plunged erratically. Often she was on her beam ends, fighting for leverage against the pounding waters. At other times she was swept sideways, tacking to port or starboard. Her timbers squeaked in agony; her masts, stripped of canvas, tilted and swayed with the violent pitching of the ship.

In the steerage the miserable immigrants huddled like animals in a pen. Most of them were seasick, and the entire area accommodating the 65 passengers stank of sour vomit. Many were wide-eyed with fear as the ship swung sickeningly up, then down, then sideways. Some spent long hours on their knees praying. But they stayed in their miserable quarters below, none daring to venture on deck for fear of being swept into the sea.

The crew knew, if the passengers didn't, that the unceasing storms were adding days to the crossing. The *William Brown* was forced by conditions to travel under shortened sail day after day, and this slowed their progress to a crawl. It also extended the agony of those on board.

On April 19, after approximately five weeks at sea, the storms at last diminished, but a new hazard took their place. A thick fog moved in to envelop the ship, and, because visibility was bad, she had to continue under shortened sail.

Most of those in steerage were unaware of the fog. All they knew was that the frantic heaving of the ship had quieted, and they tried as best they could to sleep and thereby ease their shattered nerves. Thus it was that most of the passengers and part of the crew were in their bunks as the midnight hour approached, unsuspecting that danger was now closer at hand than it had been during the most violent storms.

It was at this moment of unguarded ease that the *William Brown* hit the iceberg. The suddenly stricken ship rode up the side of the big berg as if trying to climb it, then slid off. Captain Harris, suspecting the worst, commanded the crew to start manning the pumps. As the ship listed drunkenly to port, a sailor rushed up from below to confirm the captain's fears.

"There's a big hole forward, sir," he said.

"How big?"

"Maybe six feet across, sir."

Captain Harris went with the sailor to inspect the damage to the ship. His face blanched. A jagged hole had been opened in the bow of the *William Brown*, measuring about six feet high and three feet wide. There was no doubt about it. The ship was doomed.

Captain Harris rushed back to the deck to find complete disorder. The frightened passengers, rudely awakened from their sleep, were milling about aimlessly. All were scantily clad: a few men wore trousers, others sleeping garments, and the women wore coats over their nightgowns. Utter confusion reigned. The passengers were talking loudly and screaming as the seriousness of their plight dawned on them. Crewmen were racing around, trying to calm the immigrants. Mates Rhodes and Parker had released the lifeboats from their davits, swinging them over the sides preparatory to lowering them. The problem was that only two lifeboats were available—a longboat and a smaller jollyboat. There would not be enough room in these two craft to take all the passengers and the crew.

Captain Harris knew this and apparently the terrified passengers sensed it, for as soon as the longboat was lowered there was a mad rush to get into it. Within minutes the boat was overloaded with struggling humanity—a tangled heap of men, women, and children.

The captain tried desperately to bring order out of chaos. He ordered first mate Rhodes to take charge of the longboat and assigned second mate Parker to the jollyboat. Parker was able to lower the jollyboat with less trouble, since most of the passengers had overlooked the little boat at the stern of the ship in their hysterical attempt to get into the longboat. When the jollyboat was lowered into the water, Parker, six crewmen, and one woman passenger were in it.

Captain Harris, leaning over the rail, shouted commands to Parker.

"Put over a rope to the longboat," he ordered. "Tie the two together and get away from the ship."

Parker did as he was told, and the sorely pressed captain turned to face 31 others who were still on the *William Brown* with no means of getting off.

"Save us, Captain, save us!" The words rang in his ears. There was no way he could do this. The *William Brown* would go down in a short time now, and those aboard would be lost. There was no way to prevent it.

From the jollyboat in the water Captain Harris heard the frantic voice of Parker.

"For God's sake, Captain, get off! The ship will be going down any minute!"

Captain Harris took a deep breath. There seemed no

reason for him to stay aboard. He could not help the
remaining 31 passengers, but he could help himself. With
a quick movement he broke away from the passengers
beseeching him to save them, slid down the davit ropes,
and tumbled into the jollyboat.

Captain Harris sat with his head bowed, the anguished
cries of those left aboard the ship grating on his ears and
his conscience. He held his hands to his ears, but he could
not blot out the sounds of their voices.

"Take us with you, Captain! Have mercy!"

The crew members bent to the oars, and the two boats
drifted a safe distance away from the sinking ship.
Through the fog the ship appeared as a misty blur, but it
was obvious that the bow was settling deeper in the water
and that at any moment the ship would plunge to the
bottom.

It seemed an eternity but was only a half hour later
when the *William Brown* slowly disappeared beneath
the inky waters, carrying with her the 31 passengers left
aboard.

That was the finish for the *William Brown*, but only the
beginning for the nine people in the jollyboat (built for
seven) and the 42 who were jammed in the longboat
(capacity 18). Of the 42 in the longboat, nine were members of the crew. Of the nine in the jollyboat, eight were
crewmen. Thus the 17 crewmen had all escaped the sinking ship, but 31 passengers had perished.

Those who had made the lifeboats were but little better
off. The night was dark, the temperature frigid. None of
the survivors were warmly dressed, and the people
pressed together to give each other the benefit of their
body warmth. The fog was dense, and the boats could do
nothing but drift hopelessly in the Stygian night, trying to
avoid another collision with the icebergs that were all
around them. And, worst of all, the two boats, tiny specks

in a giant ocean, were 250 miles from land. The experienced seamen—Harris, Rhodes, Parker, and Holmes—knew the truth if the others did not. They would never be able to reach land on their own. The only possibility was rescue by another ship, and the fog, if it persisted, made that unlikely.

For six long, painful hours the boats drifted in total darkness. In the morning, much to the relief of the castaways, the sun temporarily burned off the fog. But it was the only bright spot in their predicament. No rescue ship showed her sail on the horizon. The jollyboat was leaking, and constant bailing was necessary. The longboat was even worse off. Overloaded with cold and numb passengers, it was barely afloat. It rode so low in the water that the sea lapped at its gunwales. Every time a wave rocked the boat, water would rush in and drench the passengers, and the crowded condition of the boat made bailing extremely difficult.

Captain Harris, in the jollyboat, surveyed the situation and made a decision. He called to Rhodes who was in charge of the longboat.

"I'm going to cut the boats loose from each other," he said. "I think we'll both have a better chance if we go it alone."

Harris didn't answer for a moment; then he said, "Can't you take some of our passengers, sir? We're overloaded to the point of sinking."

Captain Harris shook his head. "Impossible. We have two more people than the jollyboat's capacity now."

A wave rocked the boats, and water poured in on the longboat's passengers again.

"See, sir?" Rhodes said in hushed tones. "We're so low in the water that we're going to sink. We're going to have to do something about it. You understand what I mean, don't you, Captain?"

For several moments the captain stared at Rhodes. "I know what you mean, Rhodes," he said in an undertone. "I'm putting you in complete charge of the longboat. Do what you have to do, *but only as a last resort*."

Then he addressed the crewmen in the longboat. "I'm placing first mate Rhodes in full command," he said. "Obey him as you would me."

Rhodes appeared stunned by the captain's edict. As the ropes were cast off, he sat in the stern of the longboat staring into space. The captain's words tugged at his sanity. *Do what you have to do, but only as a last resort.*

As Rhodes sat there in shocked silence he heard seaman Holmes giving orders to the crew about the scanty provisions aboard and instructions to the passengers on how to bail. A feeling of relief swept over him. He hated the responsibility that had been thrust upon him, and he was glad that Holmes was showing leadership qualities and assuming some of the duties for him.

The day in the longboat passed without incident, except that the sun disappeared again, and an icy rain fell, making the huddled passengers even more miserable. When night came the fog returned, and the unhappy survivors steeled themselves for another night of misery.

It was worse than anyone had expected. With the darkness came a rising wind, and the boat rocked perilously in heavy swells. Under cover of the night Rhodes called Holmes and a huge black seaman named James Murray to his side. In hushed tones he discussed what might have to be done. If it became obvious that all were going to perish, then some of the passengers would have to be jettisoned to save the others.

"There is no other way," Holmes agreed.

"I'll bear the responsibility for giving the order," Rhodes said. "As Captain Harris said, it will be only as a last resort."

That "last resort" came during the night. The winds stirred the sea to a frenzy, and several times the longboat almost capsized. Then, suddenly, a huge wave broke over the boat, filling it with water.

"We're going to sink!" someone shouted.

Rhodes gritted his teeth. He looked at Holmes and Murray. The time had come.

"It's got to be done," he said. "Get to work, men— lighten the boat."

Holmes and Murray hesitated only a moment, then moved toward a man lying close to them.

"Stand up," Holmes said.

The man scrambled to his feet, fright in his eyes. He knew their intention, and he intended to fight them off. There was a brief struggle, but he was no match for the two muscular seamen. Holmes finally grabbed him and lifted him off his feet. With a grunt he shoved the man overboard. In the blackness of the night there was a splash. The women in the boat screamed.

Holmes and Murray moved to the next man. There was no order or reason to their selection. The next man closest to where they stood was automatically the victim.

This man also struggled. "I've got a wife and three children," he cried. "In the name of God, spare me!"

But Holmes and Murray hardened themselves against such pleas. Again there was a great cry of fright and agony as the man was tossed into the sea. Again there was the deadly splash, and the cries and sobs of other passengers that followed.

The next victim went with a sort of resigned willingness.

"Give me five minutes to pray," he said somberly.

Holmes nodded. The two seamen stood idly by as the man prayed, and when he was finished they picked him up and threw him overboard.

Holmes selected a fourth victim but let him go when

Rhodes objected. "His wife is here with him," he said. "You cannot part man and wife."

Holmes and Murray pulled another man to his feet, and this time they found themselves the center of a hornet's nest. The man had two sisters in the boat, and they fought like enraged beasts to save their brother. They scratched and clawed at the two seamen and tried to pull their brother back in the boat with them.

"If you throw him over," they cried, "we'll go too!"

They were as good as their word. When Holmes finally bested them and threw the man overboard, the two sisters leaped into the water to drown with their brother.

Before the terrible orgy ended fourteen people were thrown overboard to lighten the longboat.

A fog-shrouded dawn finally broke upon the scene. The 28 wretches still left in the longboat lay like trapped animals, their eyes glued to Holmes, Murray, and Rhodes. Daylight revealed that the boat was not shipping as much water now, but it was still riding low in the sea.

Rhodes sat in the stern of the boat with his face in his hands. The grisly murders had shaken him badly. When Holmes said softly to him, "She's still riding too low in the water. Two more ought to go," Rhodes said, "Oh, my God!" But he did not forbid the act.

Holmes and Murray moved quickly, seizing two men who lay listlessly in the bottom of the boat and tossed them over the side.

Sixteen had now been killed. Only 26 remained. None of the nine crewmen had been sacrificed—only passengers!

Holmes, a basically decent man, felt the same twinges of regret and guilt experienced by Rhodes at having performed the foul deed of murder on the high seas. But he knew that if he had not acted as he had, they would all, by this time, be in Davy Jones's locker.

In an attempt to make some sort of amends, Holmes

took an oar and a coat and made a makeshift mast and sail. He did not really think it would do much good. They were still more than 200 miles from shore, and there was little chance that a ship would spot their mast and rescue them.

But for once luck was with them. On the third day following the sinking of the *William Brown*, Holmes spotted a ship in the distance. Grabbing a shawl from one of the women, he waved it frantically. For long moments there was uncertainty as to whether or not the ship had sighted them, but at last the vessel seemed to be moving in their direction.

"She sees us!" Holmes cried. "She's coming about!"

The ship was the schooner *Crescent*, out of New York and bound for Le Havre, France. She picked up the survivors and continued to Le Havre. After proper rest in the French city, the passengers and crew of the *William Brown* returned to the United States. It was then that they learned that Captain Harris and the jollyboat also had been fortunate. They had been rescued by the French fishing lugger *La Mere de Familie* six days after the wreck of the *William Brown*.

But the saga of the *William Brown* was not over. The tragic story of the sinking and the aftermath of murder swept the United States. Public opinion was aroused. Newspapers kept the story aflame with articles and editorials. From warm and safe offices newspaper reporters who had never experienced the perils of the sea wrote indignant editorials. They condemned the officers of the ship, along with Holmes and Murray, for "wholesale murder of innocent people" and contended that it was the duty of the crew to protect the passengers rather than sacrifice them with "callous inhumanity." One salient point that was hammered home was the fact that only passengers had been tossed from the longboat—not one crew member had been sacrificed.

On August 14, 1841, the U.S. government issued warrants charging the longboat crew with murder. But curiously, Holmes was the only one indicted under the act of April 30, 1790, which provided punishment for any sailor committing homicide on the high seas. A U.S. attorney in Philadelphia, William Meredith, was apparently willing to use Holmes as the scapegoat in the case, for he failed to locate and bring to trial anyone else.

Captain Harris and first mate Rhodes had returned to sea on a schooner plying South American waters, and, despite the fact that they were the ones who gave the fatal order to sacrifice passengers, Meredith had merely taken their depositions and let them go. Second mate Parker, who had witnessed the conversation between Rhodes and Captain Harris, had disappeared, and no attempt was made to find him. James Murray, who had aided Holmes in throwing over the passengers, had faded from sight and no effort was made to find him, either. Holmes, alone, took the blame.

Holmes spent seven months in jail awaiting his trial, and on April 13, 1842, the case of *United States* v. *Alexander William Holmes* was tried before Justice Henry Baldwin of the U.S. Circuit Court at Philadelphia. The sensational trial intrigued the entire nation. It was more than a murder trial. A great principle hung in the balance. The question that would be decided, perhaps for all time, was the exact relationship between passengers and crew during moments of danger at sea.

Seven survivors of the longboat disaster took the stand to tell their versions of the tragedy. Some condemned Holmes for his actions; others supported them as "necessary under the conditions." But it was noted that none of them were completely without sympathy for Holmes. Since the government had mysteriously avoided bringing Captain Harris and first mate Rhodes to the stand and had made no real effort to find the missing Parker or Murray,

sympathy in general seemed to shift to Holmes. The
feeling that he was being made a scapegoat rested uneas-
ily on their consciences, and the basic unfairness of the
situation rankled them. Before long the newspapers were
echoing the same sentiments.

When the case was at last ready for the jury, the pros-
ecutor thundered that their decision would live forever
in the annals of the sea, either justifying or condemning
the kind of murderous action committed by the prisoner
at the bar. The defense maintained that Holmes' action
was justified because, had he permitted all passengers to
remain in the longboat, all 42 of them would have not
seen morning.

As the jury pondered the case, the nation waited impatiently for their decision. For sixteen hours they deliber-
ated, and when they returned to the courtroom, the foreman announced that they had been unable to agree.

Justice Henry Baldwin sent them back to the jury room
to try again. Ten hours passed before they again returned.
This time they had a verdict. Holmes was guilty of man-
slaughter, but the recommendation was that the court
show mercy.

Holmes was liable for a fine of $1,000 and three years in
jail, but the court complied with the jury's recommendation for mercy by sentencing him to only six months and
tacking on a ludicrous fine of $20.

That seemed to satisfy everyone. Editorial comment in
the press was almost unanimous that the sentence was
fair, but it was pointed out that Holmes, having been
made a scapegoat for the others, deserved a pardon. The
newspapers condemned Captain Harris for deserting his
passengers by leaving the *William Brown* with 31 still on
board and by ordering Rhodes to sacrifice the passengers
in the longboat "as a last resort." They also censured the
ship owners for not providing enough lifeboats and the
government for not demanding that they do so.

As far as the court was concerned, the case was closed—even though the government never did explain why it had not located and prosecuted Harris, Rhodes, Parker, and Murray. Friends of Holmes, who felt he had been singled out unfairly, drew up a petition asking President John Tyler to pardon him. In addition, letters from all over the country poured into the White House. But the President refused to intercede, and Holmes served his six months in prison. When he was released, he went back to sea and never again figured in a controversy.

Whatever the deficiencies in the trial itself, it established one enduring principle: In moments of peril at sea, no person, regardless of necessity, has the right to take another's life.

That principle still endures as a barrier against a repetition of the gruesome murders that followed the demise of the *William Brown*.

5

Discipline on the
Birkenhead (1852)

W<small>HEN</small> a British ship meets trouble on the high seas, it is almost inevitable that an officer or crew member will shout the three magic words that have been an inspiration to the country's seafarers for more than a century.

"Remember the *Birken'ead!*"

This rallying cry is intended to stiffen the backbone and inspire discipline during perilous moments on the waters of the world, and there is every evidence that it has done just that on numerous occasions. The *Birkenhead* (pronounced *Birken'ead* by h-dropping Englishmen) was a troopship that went down off the coast of Africa, and, because of the courageous action of those who were forced to go down with the ship, the incident has become the classic example of discipline at sea. In fact, the *Birkenhead* set the pattern for the order of rescue from a sinking ship—women and children first—that has endured to this day.

The year was 1852. The British Empire, under Queen Victoria, was at its height, but like all empires it had to be held together by the military. At the moment, Britain was busy trying to tame the Kaffirs, a tribe in South Africa who had some strange idea that independence was preferable to rule by the British. What had started as a fringe uprising, however, had escalated into a larger war because the Kaffirs proved to be stalwart and very stubborn warriors. As a result, reinforcements were needed, and Her Majesty's Steamship *Birkenhead* was chosen to transport troops, and in some cases their families, to the threatened colony.

The H.M.S. *Birkenhead*, built in 1845, was well-suited to the job. She was a 1,400-ton, iron-hulled paddle-wheel steamer that, like all steamers of the day, also carried canvas. She was intended to serve as a frigate but was commissioned as a troop-carrier instead. On January 2, 1852, this "finest transport in the Royal Navy" left the British Isles bound for Cape Town and Algoa Bay at the Cape of Good Hope. More than 800 passengers were aboard.

The *Birkenhead*'s first stop was Simon's Bay, where she lay for two days to be reprovisioned and to disembark more than 100 soldiers and their families. When she left, bound for Algoa Bay on the southeastern coast of the Cape of Good Hope, she carried 630 people: 130 Royal Marines, 480 officers and soldiers from the Queen's Regiment, the 12th Lancers, the 43rd, 73rd, 74th, and 91st Regiments, and 20 women and children who made up the families of some of the officers and soldiers.

Under the command of Captain Robert Salmond, the *Birkenhead* sailed from Simon's Bay on February 25, 1852, her bowsprit pointed toward Algoa Bay. Captain Salmond set a prudent course some four miles offshore to avoid the reefs in the area, but during the night the ship strayed somewhat closer to the African shoreline than was planned.

It was two o'clock on the morning of February 26 when the disaster occurred. Most of the passengers were asleep, and the *Birkenhead* was steaming along at a rate of 8½ knots an hour. The weather was clear, the sea smooth, and there seemed to be no danger in sight. But suddenly the ship lurched crazily as it struck a rocky reef and came to a shuddering stop. The *Birkenhead* was grounded about three miles off Point Danger, a formidable section of the African coastline.

Although most of the passengers were awakened from sound sleeps, within minutes of the crash the decks swarmed with soldiers, sailors, officers and the wives and children aboard. Even though the extent of the damage to the *Birkenhead* was not immediately known, the abrupt halt to the ship's progress and the grinding noise as she hit the reef was adequate testimony to those who knew the sea that the ship was in dire trouble.

Captain Salmond, stirred from his bed, rushed to the deck half-dressed. He went directly to the officer of the watch.

"What has happened?" he demanded.

"We've grounded, sir," was the reply.

"What course were you steering?"

"SSE ½ E, sir."

Captain Salmond noted that this was correct, thereby absolving the officer of the watch of any blame. For a minute or two the captain seemed undecided about his course of action, and during that time a tragedy was taking place below. The *Birkenhead* had struck a rock just aft of the foremast, opening a giant hole in the hull. The water had rushed in with such force that it had drowned 100 men in their hammocks almost before they could move.

Now the hold was filling with water, and the fires beneath the boilers were in danger of being extinguished.

Captain Salmond ordered depth soundings be taken at once. The soundings revealed that there were but two fathoms of water at the bow, seven alongside the ship, and eleven at the stern.

It was then that Captain Salmond gave a command that he thought might take the ship off the reef safely. He asked for a back turn. The engines were reversed, and the paddle-wheels on port and starboard chugged backwards. For one tense moment the ship trembled on the reef, then there was another grinding noise as she moved backward—just enough to open another mammoth hole in the hull.

Water rushed in to extinguish the boilers as the *Birkenhead* slid clear of the reef into deeper water. There was no doubt, then, in the minds of Captain Salmond or the crew. The ship was sinking rapidly.

There is often chaos on the deck of a ship facing disaster, but in the case of the *Birkenhead* a great discipline and silence reigned. This was the work of Major Seton, the ranking British officer aboard, who called all other officers to a hasty conference.

"There must be order and silence among the men," he told them. "It is up to you to enforce this rule." He turned to Captain Edward Wright of the 91st Regiment. "Captain Salmond is the commander of this ship. You are to take orders from him and have all of his wishes executed immediately."

What happened thereafter has become known as "the *Birkenhead* drill"—the word "drill," as used by the British, signifying discipline. The troops stood in silent ranks before Captain Wright, at attention and awaiting orders. The orders came fast, and the men moved to execute them. Sixty men were dispatched to the chain pumps on the lower afterdeck, and they marched to their tasks as if on parade. Another sixty were ordered to the paddle-box lifeboats, and these boats and a large cutter were made ready for evacuation.

The *Birkenhead*, filling rapidly with water, was now rolling heavily, and down below the officers' horses were creating havoc. Captain Salmond decided to jettison the horses to ease the plight of the ship. Soldiers of the 12th Lancers were dispatched to pitch the horses out of the port gangway, and again the selected soldiers marched to their duty silently and efficiently. As soon as the horses were over the side, swimming instinctively toward shore, the women and children were carefully loaded into the cutter. Master's Assistant Richards was put in charge of the cutter and told to stand off from the ship at about 150 yards.

Meanwhile, the crew was making attempts to lower other boats, but without much luck. Wreckage caused when the *Birkenhead* grounded had destroyed a pinnace amidships, and when an attempt was made to lower a port boat, the tackle broke and it fell, crushing several men and depositing others into the water. They tried to lower a gig and another cutter but found the pins in the davits so rusted that they could not be loosened, and it was impossible to lower the longboat on its complicated tackle system in the time they had to accomplish the task. Consequently, the three boats successfully launched held between 60 and 70 people. The others—crewmen and soldiers—were still aboard the *Birkenhead*, still standing in ranks, still motionless and silent, accepting whatever fate was in store for them.

In a somewhat useless desperation, other members of the crew fired rockets into the sky to attract any ship that might be nearby, but they knew this was a forlorn hope since marine traffic in the area was light.

As it turned out, the cutter carrying the women and children was in the safest position, 150 yards away from the stricken *Birkenhead*. It was only minutes after the cutter was launched that a second step in the inexorable march to tragedy occurred when, with a ripping noise, the entire bow of the *Birkenhead* broke off at the foremast, the bowsprit rising in the air toward the foretopmast. The huge funnel, its stays parting, crashed down on the starboard paddle-box, killing the men working to lower the boat and sweeping the paddle-box and the lifeboat into the sea.

Only 12 minutes had passed since the moment the *Birkenhead* first struck the submerged rock—and already the ship was breaking up.

Captain Salmond ordered Wright to move the troops aft to the poop. At the command the troops marched smartly to their new positions. It was hoped that the weight of the men at the stern would counterbalance the tendency of the forepart of the ship to sink, but the chances of success were slim. As they stood quietly and steadily in their ranks, the troops must have known how slim those chances were. All lifeboats that could be lowered were now full and away from the ship. Those who remained aboard must go down with the ship—it was that simple. If they did not immediately drown in the waters, a great school of sharks, which were hungrily circling, would finish them off quickly. Despite this horrible fate, the troops did not panic but stood like emotionless automatons before their officers.

As the men calmly awaited their doom, a second incident speeded the end of the *Birkenhead*. Suddenly the ship, or what remained of it, broke in two again, just aft of the mainmast, hurling a large number of the men into the sea. Ensign Lucas of the 73rd Regiment described the scene in the water after his rescue. "A dreadful sight it was. Some men were in their last dying efforts, others were striking out manfully and suddenly going down with a yell of agony—their shrieks seem still to ring in my ears—some were pulling others down in their efforts to keep above water."

The poop and afterdeck stayed afloat for a few minutes, and incredibly the soldiers still held their ranks, knowing now the end was near. Ensign Lucas happened to be standing near Major Seton and he held out his hand.

"I hope that we meet ashore, sir," he said.

Seton smiled wryly. "I do not think we shall, Lucas, as I cannot swim a stroke," he replied.

The commander of a ship usually knows the precise moment when his vessel is ready to go down, and seconds before the stern rose in the air prior to its death plunge, Captain Salmond issued an ill-conceived order.

"All those able to swim take to the water and try to reach the lifeboats!" he cried.

Immediately the order was rescinded by Major Seton and Captain Wright. They realized that if the soldiers obeyed this order the three lifeboats would be swamped, and all would perish.

"Stand fast!" came the order from Captain Wright. "Do not imperil the safety of the women and children in the lifeboats!"

And the soldiers obediently held their ranks.

Slowly, as if in utter despair, the stern of the ship sank, and the men grimly held their stations as the water rose around them. They went down with the ship with almost stoic indifference. Only when the water rose above their heads did they break ranks and start to swim in an effort to save themselves.

When the *Birkenhead* finally settled on the bottom, a portion of the main topmast protruded from the water. About 50 men decided their best chance of rescue was to climb the topmast, cling to the rigging, and wait for the arrival of another ship to rescue them. Some of the men held onto their precarious positions all night long, but others were too weak and fatigued and fell into the sea.

Most of the men were now in the water, and of these the majority perished. Among the victims were Major Seton and Captain Salmond. Those who could not swim went down immediately. Those who could swim headed for shore, but either became exhausted and drowned or were caught in a tangle of kelp near shore and dragged under. Many were attacked by sharks, leaving only tinges of blood on the water to mark their end. Some of the men clung to the wreckage of the ship, hoping that some miracle would save them.

Captain Wright was one of the men who clung to wreckage in the sea. In his later report to the Commandant of Cape Town, he wrote:

> I think there must have been about 200 on the driftwood. I was on a large piece along with five others, and we picked up nine or ten more. The swell carried the wood in the direction of Point Danger. As soon as it got to the weeds and breakers, finding that it would not support all that were on it, I jumped off and swam on shore; and when the others, and also those that were on the other pieces of wood, reached the shore, we proceeded into the country, to try to find a habitation of any sort, where we could obtain shelter.
>
> Many of the men were naked, and almost all without shoes. Owing to the country, being covered with thick, thorny bushes, our progress was slow, but after walking till about 3 p.m. we came to where a wagon was outspanned, and the driver of it directed us to a small bay, where there is a hut of a fisherman. The bay is called Stanford's Cove. We arrived there about sunset, and as the men had nothing to eat, I went on to a farm house, about eight or nine miles from the Cove, and sent back provisions for that day. The next morning I sent another day's provisions, and the men were removed up to a farm of Captain Smale's, about 12 or 14 miles up the

country. Lieutenant Girardot, of the 43rd, and Cornet Bond, of the 12th Lancers, accompanied this party, which amounted to 68 men, including 18 sailors.

Meanwhile, the people in the lifeboats were having better luck. Because of the heavy surf and the possibility of being mired in the kelp in the dark of night, they could not safely bring the boats into shore. Wisely they let them drift about until daylight. In the morning they spotted a schooner in the distance and flagged it down. She proved to be the *Lioness*. A rescue operation that lasted several hours saved all those in the boats and those who had managed to cling to the rigging of the *Birkenhead* during the long night.

Captain Wright turned out to be one of the most heroic of the survivors. Despite his own exhaustion, he went back to the scene of the wreck and traveled 20 miles up and down the coast searching for possible survivors. For three days he kept up the search. His report says:

> I fortunately fell in with the crew of a whaleboat that is employed sealing on Dyer's Island. I got them to take the boat outside the seaweed, whilst I went along the shore. The seaweed on the coast is very thick and of immense strength, so that it would have caught most of the driftwood. Happily, the boat picked up two men, and I also found two. Although they were all much exhausted, two of them having been in the water thirty-eight hours, they were all right the next day, except a few bruises. It was eighty-six hours, on Sunday afternoon when I left the coast, since the wreck had taken place; and as I had carefully examined every part of the rocks, and also sent the whaleboat over to Dyer's Island, I can safely assert that when I left there was not a living soul on the coast of those that had been on board the ill-fated *Birkenhead*.

Later Captain Wright returned with others to the coast and buried all bodies that had been washed ashore, a gruesome but necessary task. This group of searchers also found five horses that had made it to shore. One of them belonged to Captain Wright.

Estimates of the number of *Birkenhead* casualties differ: one source lists 454 dead; another says 445 were lost and 193 saved; still another claims 420 died, and 210 were rescued. Since most sources agree that 630 persons were aboard the *Birkenhead* when it left Simon's Bay for Algoa Bay, the figures of 420 lost and 210 saved at least add up and seem to be correct.

Despite all the evidence of strict discipline during the sinking of the *Birkenhead*, there are some who believe that the bravery shown by the troops who stood at attention until the ship sank is open to question. They feel that the men did not know the ship was in imminent danger of sinking and that their seeming indifference stemmed from ignorance. But it seems likely that when the bow of the ship broke off, followed later by a break at the center of the ship, most men must have realized the peril they faced. Captain Wright, in his report, had glowing words for the conduct of the troops.

> The order and regularity that prevailed on board, from the time the ship struck till she totally disappeared, far exceeded anything that I thought could be effected by the best discipline; and it is the more to be wondered at, seeing that most of the soldiers were but a short time in the service. Every one of them did as he was directed, and there was not a murmur or a cry amongst them, until the vessel made her final plunge. I could not name any individual officer who did more than another. All received their orders, and had them carried out, as if the men were embarking instead of going to the bottom; there was only this difference, that I never saw any embarcation conducted with so little noise or confusion.

Although the *Birkenhead* sank well over a century ago, it still lives as the prime example of discipline under stress at sea. There is little doubt that the way the *Birkenhead* disaster was handled has had its effect on the minds of seagoing men ever since.

An example occurred 102 years later, on March 28, 1954, when another British troopship, the *Empire Windrush*, met disaster in the Mediterranean. She was 50 miles off the coast of Algeria when a boiler exploded. There were 1,515 persons aboard, many of them service men and their families coming home from the Far East.

Even though it was obvious that not all the people on board could make the lifeboats, there was no panic. Colonel Robert Scott, commander of the troops on board, saw to that. Through a megaphone came this message:

"This is the *Birken'ead* drill! Stand fast on deck! Wait until you are assigned a boat."

The *Birkenhead* drill was carried out by the crew and the soldiers with every bit as much courage as those on the *Birkenhead* had shown a century before. The crew stayed at the various posts assigned to them, and the soldiers stood at attention before their officers. Women and children were helped into the lifeboats, along with 17 invalids, and when this was accomplished it became evident that there was room in the boats for a few of the men. Some would be lucky; others not.

The choice was made easily. An old rule used by the British in such emergencies was enforced by the officers.

"Funeral order!" was the command. "The youngest go first."

Officers moved down the line of soldiers and selected the younger men. The boats were lowered into the water. There were still some 300 soldiers on board the *Empire Windrush*.

The crew began to throw over chairs, kegs, boarding, and other floatable material for the men to cling to in the water. Then Colonel Scott gave the command: "Remove clothing and shoes and go over the side. *But do not swim to a lifeboat!"*

When the men had all gone over the side, Colonel Scott followed—the last man to leave the flaming ship.

Not one man in the water made an attempt to reach a lifeboat, even though they were temptingly close. Their discipline was generously rewarded when a freighter hove into view and picked up both those in the lifeboats and the swimmers.

Other than four men who were killed by the explosion, not one life was lost as the *Empire Windrush* sank to the bottom. The *Birkenhead* drill had been followed to the letter.

There have been other examples. The *Birkenhead* drill was again employed in the sinking of the British liner *Republic*, which went down off Nantucket without loss of life. A British freighter, *Templemore*, was swept by fire off the coast of Virginia, and the discipline inherent in the *Birkenhead* drill again served its purpose when all of the crew were saved.

Then there was the *Titanic* that struck an iceberg and sank in the North Atlantic in 1912 with a disastrous death toll of 1,517. Yet the massed people on board honored the rule of "women and children first" and sang hymns as the ship went down.

Great Britain has never forgotten the discipline exhibited on the *Birkenhead* in 1852. It has become a memorable part of British sea lore and has been immortalized by the famous English author, Rudyard Kipling, in "Soldier an' Sailor, Too" from *The Seven Seas*, with these words:

> To take your chance in the thick of the rush,
>> with firing all about,
>
> Is nothing so bad when you've cover to 'and,
>> an' leavin' an' likin' to shout;

But to stand an' be still to the Birken'ead drill
    is a damn tough bullet to chew,

An' they done it, the Jollies—'Er Majesty's
    Jollies—soldier an' sailor too!

Their work was done when it 'adn't begun; they
    was younger nor me an' you;

Their choice it was plain between drownin' in
    'eaps an' being mashed by the screw,

So they stood an' was still to the Birken'ead
    drill, soldier an' sailor too!

6

The *Atlantic:* Death at
Mars Head (1873)

Fᴏʀ months after the luxury liner *Atlantic*
smashed herself to bits on the wild and rocky southern
shore of Nova Scotia, mariners who knew the inside story
called it "the crime of the century." It was hardly less
than that, for 481 persons lost their lives in what is considered the worst maritime disaster ever to occur on the
mainland of the North American continent. The criminal
aspect of the tragedy was the fact that the *Atlantic* was
destroyed not because of heavy weather or a fog-
shrouded coast but because of gross negligence on the
part of the steamship company and the incredible blun-
dering of the ship's captain.

It was shortly after three o'clock in the morning, under
a clear sky studded with stars, that the 3,707-ton trans-
atlantic liner rammed ashore at a point known as Mars
Head. Within minutes water gushed into the bowels of
the ship, and she heeled hard to port. In a short time

hundreds of passengers trapped in steerage perished as they tried to reach companionways, and hundreds who made the decks slid from the listing ship into the sea.

The *Atlantic* had run ashore nineteen miles from the entrance to Halifax Harbor because the ship's captain had charted her course carelessly, had placed the ship in the hands of subordinate officers and had retired to his cabin. The captain was asleep at the moment of impact.

The steamship *Atlantic*, one of the finest passengers ships in the White Star Line, sailed from Liverpool, England, on March 20, 1873, making a one-day stop at the Irish port of Queenstown (now Cobh) to take on mail and steerage passengers before steaming into the broad Atlantic bound for New York. She was a magnificent ship for her time, 435 feet long and with elegant public rooms that marked her as one of the most prestigious luxury liners afloat. She was well-constructed of angle iron, had three eight-foot high decks, and boasted seven watertight compartments. Her four engines were capable of propelling her across the Atlantic at speeds of twelve to fifteen knots per hour. In the unlikely event of engine failure, however, the *Atlantic* could be quickly converted to a sailing vessel, since she was equipped with four masts, the mainmast towering 150 feet above the sea.

Captain John A. Williams, a portly Englishman, was her commander, and he was considered to be one of the most competent officers sailing the Atlantic. Officers subordinate to him included Chief Officer John W. Firth, Second Officer Henry Metcalf, Third Officer Cornelius Brady, and Fourth Officer John Brown.

Aboard the *Atlantic* on what was to be her final voyage were 931 persons—a large percentage of them women and children.

The journey began well, with fine weather for the first

few days of the trip. On the 24th of March, however, the weather worsened, and Captain Williams was forced to reduce the speed of his ship from a satisfactory eight knots an hour to five. For three days the *Atlantic* labored against heavy headwinds, and on March 26 the captain observed that her supply of coal was being consumed at an alarming rate. The engineer's report on that date showed but 319 tons aboard, and Captain Williams estimated that the ship was about 1,130 miles from Sandy Hook.

The *Atlantic* continued along at cautiously reduced speeds until the 31st of March, at which time the coal supply had been reduced to 127 tons, and the ship still had 460 miles to go to reach Sandy Hook. The *Atlantic* had devoured 192 tons of coal traveling 670 miles, and Captain Williams decided that traveling another 460 miles on 127 tons of coal was stretching the risk to the breaking point.

It was then that the captain made a critical decision. As he later explained,

> As the ship by this time was making but seven knots an hour, the wind being at the southwest, the glass falling, and a westerly swell on, I thought the risk too great to keep on, as, in the event of a westerly gale coming up, we might find ourselves shut out of all sources of supply. The chief steward also reported the stores short; fresh provisions enough for the saloon for two days, when all but the bread and rice would be out. At one p.m., after receiving the engineer's report, I decided to make for Sambro Island, being then north and distant 170 miles.

A lighthouse was situated at Sambro Island, near Halifax Harbor, that would safely guide the *Atlantic* into port where the ship's bunkers could be replenished with coal and other necessary provisions obtained. The decision was obviously a wise one, for it made certain the ship would not be stranded in a gale without steam up and with inadequate provisions. But after making this correct decision, Captain Williams proceeded to demolish it by making two unbelievable blunders.

The first mistake occurred at 11:55 P.M. on March 31, when Captain Williams, standing on the bridge, saw a red-tinted lighthouse beacon in the distance. Without bothering to consult his charts, the captain assumed he was looking at the Sambro Island light. Actually, what he saw was the lighthouse at Peggy's Point, which was located about twenty miles farther east on a rocky ledge jutting into the water. Had he consulted his charts, the captain would have discovered that Peggy's Point lighthouse displayed a red beam, whereas the Sambro Island light was white.

But the captain did not do this. Instead, he incorrectly charted a course that he believed would take the *Atlantic* five miles east of the Sambro Island light and into Halifax Harbor. Actually, the course was to carry him directly toward the jagged coastline guarded by the Peggy's Point light and would result in destruction of the ship and the death of more than half the persons aboard.

At 12:20 A.M. the captain made his last visit to the bridge. Third Officer Cornelius Brady was at the wheel.

"I place the ship south of Sambro," the captain said. "Keep a lookout for loose ice and keep the same course until six bells, then call me."

Captain Williams reviewed his subsequent actions later, saying:

> I then went into the chart-room and sat down. In about fifteen minutes a Mr. Fisher came in to ask some particulars about the ship, as he was writing to the Cosmopolitan (newspaper). He stayed about twenty minutes, and left. My intention was to run on until about 3 a.m. (six bells), then heave

to and await day. At midnight the ship's run was 122 miles, which would place her forty-eight miles south of Sambro; the speed by log at 12:20 being nine knots per hour.... At 12:40 my servant came up with some cocoa, but was told not to awake me until 3 a.m.

Since Captain Williams had never before entered Halifax Harbor, he should have remained on the bridge. Leaving the ship in the hands of a subordinate officer was the captain's second mistake.

At 2:00 A.M. Thomas Dunn, the quartermaster, came onto the bridge and approached Second Officer Henry Metcalf who was talking with Cornelius Brady at the wheel. Dunn sensed that they were near land, and he tried to caution Metcalf.

"I believe the ship has run its distance to make the Sambro light," he warned. "Take care and don't run aground."

Metcalf ignored him. "You're not the captain of this ship nor the mate," he said, and ordered Brady to keep the course Captain Williams had set.

Worried, Dunn went to the Fourth Officer, John Brown, but found that his opinion was not given much attention.

Meanwhile, Brady conscientiously steered the *Atlantic* toward what he believed was Halifax Harbor. The wind had by this time freshened, and the *Atlantic* was bucking a heavy swell, but there seemed no possibility of danger.

Then, shortly after 3:00 A.M., a cry came from the watchman on the bow that sent a cold chill up Brady's spine.

"Land ahead! Breakers on the starboard!"

Brady acted quickly and instinctively. He swung the wheel hard to port, but he was too late. There was a terrible crunch as the *Atlantic* struck land and tried, battering-ram fashion, to scale the rocky ledge on which she had grounded.

It was 3:15 in the morning of April 1, All Fool's Day— an ironic touch to a tragic blunder.

Captain Williams, who later claimed that he had not been called at 3:00 A.M. as he had ordered and could have averted the tragedy if he had, was awakened by the shock as the *Atlantic* grounded on the rocky promontory known as Mars Head. Donning his clothes quickly, he rushed up on deck. To his surprise he saw that huge waves were already sweeping over the ship.

But the horror that was taking place below, unknown to the captain at the time, was tragedy at its grimmest. In the steerage the startled passengers, awakened from a sound sleep and not knowing exactly what was wrong, dressed rapidly and tried to get to the companionways leading to the deck. Within minutes the stairways were jammed with human beings, piled up like logs, writhing and fighting to get onto the deck. From a jagged hole in the hull, water poured into the doomed liner, and most of the steerage passengers were drowned before they could reach even temporary safety.

Some, however, escaped the flooding of the ship. With the *Atlantic* already listing hard to port, the starboard bunks were elevated and still above water. While those in port bunks, and others trying to ascend the companion-ways, drowned, the fortunate ones who had starboard bunks escaped through the portholes and clung precari-ously to the side of the ship. One steerage passenger described his experience this way:

> I turned into my berth about 11 o'clock Monday night. The night was dark but starlit, and the weather was fine. I knew the ship was going into Halifax for coal.... I went to sleep and

woke up with a shock, and remarked to my mate, "There goes the anchor." I thought, of course, that we were safe in Halifax Harbor, but as soon as she made a second plunge I said, "My God, she's ashore!"

With that we got up and dressed. The companionway was thronged with the lower steerage passengers. Seeing that the sea was commencing to break over the ship and pour down the companionway, I got as many as possible to take to the bunks and hold on by the iron stanchions. There we remained until after daylight. The ship had fallen over and the steerage was full of water, one side only being out of it. Our only chance of escape was the ports. A number of men, probably twenty, got out through the ports to the side of the vessel. I remained until all who were alive were out. There were a great many drowned in their bunks, and others were drowned while trying to reach the ports. I got out through a port and held fast to the side of the ship for about two hours and then went to the shore by the lifeline.

The "lifeline" was the work of Cornelius Brady and quartermasters Owens and Speakman. Ten minutes after striking Mars Head, the *Atlantic* had listed so far to port that there was no possibility of lowering any of the lifeboats. Seeing the chaos on the decks, the three seamen went to the starboard side of the ship and looked out toward a huge rock that poked its head out of the sea. It seemed to be about thirty yards away from the ship.

"If we could get the passengers to that rock," Brady said, "we might save a lot of them. As things are now, we're going to lose everyone."

Finally an idea hit him. "Get me a hundred feet of line," he said. "I'll try to swim to the rock with it."

"Let me try it," Owens said. "I'm a strong swimmer."

It was a turbulent sea that Owens leaped into with the line tied around his waist. With some effort he reached the rock, but he found he could not climb out of the water.

The incessant waves kept pulling him back, and the other two men finally had to haul him back to the ship.

"I'll try it," said Speakman.

Speakman was luckier. He managed to scramble up the rock. The two men on deck then fastened a strong cable to the end of the line, and Speakman pulled it to the rock where he fastened it securely.

The rescue operation was simple in plan but difficult to execute. Fashioning a sling and pulley arrangement, Brady placed passengers in the contraption and, swimming in the water, pushed them along until they reached the rock, where they were hauled to safety by Speakman. When Brady was exhausted by his efforts, others took over.

Each time it was a violent fight against the raging sea. On some occasions the rescue device did not work, and the passenger was hurled from the makeshift sling and drowned. But many made the distance to the rock safely.

This hazardous rescue attempt was slow, and some of the passengers, wary of the makeshift lifeline, sought other places of safety. Many of them climbed into the rigging of the ship on the theory that if the ship went down, the masts would most likely protrude above the water.

Captain Williams helped in this strategy. The port lifeboats had been swept into the sea, but the starboard lifeboats were still in place. His first impulse was to place two women, who were pleading for help, in one of them. When he realized the boats could not be lowered because the ship was listing so far to port, he carried them to the main rigging and told them to hang on. "I left them," he said later, "and went aft to encourage others to go forward on the side of the ship. At this juncture the boilers exploded and the boat rolled over to leeward, the ship at this time being on her beam ends. Finding myself useless there, I went to take the ladies forward, but found them gone, nor did I see them afterward."

A wave had hurled the two women into the sea.

This incident emphasized one amazing thing about the *Atlantic* disaster. Only minutes after the ship crashed and the water rushed into the steerage, 300 crew members and passengers were dead. This included almost all of the women and children. Only a few women even reached the deck, and most of these could not hold themselves against the violence of the waves sweeping over the ship and perished in the sea. Several, however, were successful in climbing into the mizzen rigging.

Individual incidents, both of tragedy and bravery, were recorded. A lawyer named Cyrus Fisher and his wife escaped from their cabin at the initial shock and decided their best chance of eventual rescue was to climb into the rigging. As they clung to their precarious perches they both realized that their rescue was only a remote possibility, and Mrs. Fisher implored her husband to leave her and try to make his escape either by one of the boats or by way of the lifeline. He shook his head.

"I will not leave you here," he said.

But holding onto the rigging was a terrible ordeal. Waves kept sweeping over the ship, and the cold spray numbed their hands and legs, making it almost impossible for them to retain their grip. Suddenly, as a wave washed over the liner, Fisher's wife let go and was swept into the sea. At the point of exhaustion and shattered by the agony of seeing his wife disappear, Fisher let go and was thrown into the water in almost the same spot where his wife had disappeared.

Two men—Simeon Comacho, an Italian returning home to his wife and children after two years in Europe, and S. W. Vick, of Wilmington, Delaware—had desperately taken to the rigging and had held onto their insecure positions for eight hours. By that time some small boats had put out from the Nova Scotia shore to attempt rescue operations, and there was an opportunity for them to take one of the two men to safety.

Vick's body was numb with cold, and Comacho's legs were frozen and useless. The rescuers tried to take Comacho off, but he refused their help.

"Take Vick," he said. "He's in worse shape than I am. I can hang on a little longer."

Vick refused the generous offer several times, but was at last persuaded to leave. Comacho was rescued later.

Twelve-year-old John Henley was the only child rescued. When the ship struck, the boy attempted to reach the deck and found the companionways blocked by struggling humanity. His room was on the starboard side of the ship, and he returned to it, hanging on as he looked out of the open porthole. Another passenger, clinging to the side of the ship that was out of the water, reached in and pulled him out. He finally arrived safely on shore, but he lost his mother, father, and a brother in the disaster.

While all this agony was transpiring, the improvised lifeline was working efficiently. By ten o'clock in the morning 400 passengers had been rescued by the device. Some who reached the rock had managed to get to the mainland where they reported the tragedy and asked for help. Soon many boats were making their way to the stricken *Atlantic* and were removing those passengers who had managed to stay alive aboard the ship.

One of these boats was piloted by a clergyman, the Reverend Mr. Ancient, pastor of a small church on the mainland. He rescued John W. Firth, the Chief Officer of the *Atlantic*, who had managed to cling to the rigging for ten hours. Firth gratefully described the rescue this way:

> My watch ended at twelve o'clock on Monday night. The second and fourth officers took charge, and I went to my berth.

I was aroused by the shock of the vessel striking. The second officer came down to my room and said the ship was ashore, and that he was afraid she was gone. I put on a few articles of clothing, got an axe, and went up on deck to clear the boats. The ship had careened over before I reached the deck. I cleared the two starboard boats. Just then a heavy sea swept the boats away.

I was holding fast to the mizzenmast rigging and now climbed higher for safety. The night was so dark and the spray flew so thickly that we could not see well what was going on around us. I saw men on the rocks but did not know how they got there. All who were alive on board were in the rigging. When daylight came I counted thirty-two persons in the mizzenmast rigging with me, including one woman. When these saw that there were lines between the ship and the shore many of them attempted to go forward to the lines, and in doing so were washed overboard and drowned. Many reached the shore by the aid of the lines, and the fishermen's boats rescued many more. At last all had either been washed off or rescued except myself, the woman, and a boy.

The sea had become so rough that the boats could not venture near us. Soon the boy was washed off, but he swam gallantly and reached one of the boats in safety. [Although the boy is not named in Firth's account, this was obviously twelve-year-old John Henley who was rescued from his bunk by the man on the side of the boat and who later must have climbed to the rigging for safety.]

I got a firm hold of the woman and secured her in the rigging. I could see the people on shore and in the boats and could hail them, but they were unable to help us. At one o'clock in the afternoon, after we had been in the rigging for ten hours, Reverend Mr. Ancient, a Church of England clergyman, whose noble conduct I can never forget while I live, got a crew of four men to row him out to the wreck. He got into the main rigging [the deck was now under water and Mr. Ancient guided his boat directly under the rigging to which Firth clung] and threw a line to me. I caught it, made it fast around my body, and then jumped clear. A sea swept me off the wreck, but Mr. Ancient in the rescue boat held fast to the line, pulled me back and got me safely into the boat. I was then so exhausted and benumbed that I was hardly able to do anything for myself, and but for the clergyman's gallant conduct I must have perished soon.

The woman, after bearing up with remarkable strength under her great trials, had died two hours before Mr. Ancient arrived. Her half-nude body was still fast in the rigging, her eyes protruding, her mouth foaming—a terribly ghastly spectacle rendered more ghastly by the contrast with the numerous jewels that sparkled on both her hands. We had to leave her body in the rigging.

Those who escaped over the lifeline and in the rescue boats were taken in by farmers in the area until vessels were available to transfer them to more permanent shelter. Later, three ships—the *Goliath, Delta,* and *Lady Head*—took them to Halifax. For several days after the tragedy bodies were washed ashore—a total, finally, of 164, including that of a woman clinging to a baby.

Of the 931 aboard the *Atlantic*, 429 passengers and 21 crewmen were saved, and 481 lost their lives. Among the dead were 295 women and children.

An inquiry into the sinking of the *Atlantic* was ordered by the Dominion Government of Canada several days later, and some of the facts that were unearthed during the testimony placed the blame indisputably on both the White Star Line and Captain John A. Williams. In testimony delivered by Captain Williams, he said:

> I had latitude by observation and chronometer when I bore up for Halifax. The charts have all been lost. The ship increased her speed after I bore up for Halifax because we were not then so anxious to economize coal. The speed at twelve o'clock was about twelve knots. I reckoned then that we were forty-eight miles off Sambro, then bearing north, five degrees east. I considered we would pass five miles east of the Sambro ledges.

I had never before brought ships into Halifax, or been on the coast; the third officer had been in the harbor twice; none of the other officers had ever been here. I did not use the lead at all in coming to Halifax; I knew we were within soundings north of La Have; I did not sound because the night was clear and Sambro light should be seen twenty-one miles in clear weather, and in moderate weather fifteen miles; the bridge was thirty-six feet above the level of the sea. I knew I was approaching the shore; the clearness of the night and the certainty of seeing the light were my only reasons for not sounding. I am now satisfied that when I went into the chart-room I was mistaken in the locality of the ship. She must have been farther northward and westward than I thought. I knew the coast was ironbound and dangerous, though I had never been on it.

Expanding on testimony that seemed self-incriminating, Captain Williams went on:

I would not have got into forty-five fathoms of water until I was thirteen or fourteen miles south of Sambro, where I should stop the ship. If I had been sounding regularly between twelve and three o'clock, I would have been on deck, and the ship would not have gone ashore. There were three quartermasters and the second and fourth officers on deck. It was my second voyage to America in that ship. When the ship struck there was a considerable swell on. There was no sort of warning. She was going between nine and ten knots at the time.

I was too confident. I thought I knew where the vessel was. I thought that I was a long way eastward of Sambro light. To think that while hundreds of men were saved, every woman should have perished. It's horrible. If I'd been able to save just one I could bear the disaster, but to lose every woman on board, it's too terrible.

Obviously, Captain Williams bore much of the blame for the tragedy. In retrospect, it is difficult to believe that the commander of a huge passenger liner could be so uninformed as to confuse the red Peggy's Point light with the white Sambro Island light, and so utterly careless as to not check his charts to make sure he was looking at the correct beam. It is also a violation of the rules of the sea for the captain of a ship to go to sleep in his cabin when his ship is approaching a rocky and perilous shore in the dark of night—especially a shore with which he is completely unfamiliar. Captain Williams should have been on the bridge and should not have relied on subordinate officers to take the ship to Halifax safely.

Even so, the disaster would not have occurred had it not been for a penny-pinching policy on the part of the steamship company. The White Star Line had sent the *Atlantic* on her voyage with only enough coal in her bunkers and provisions in her larder to take her to New York—*if* the weather was favorable all the way. It was the practice of the White Star Line, as well as other steamship companies of the day, to gamble that the weather would be good. The theory was that if the weather turned bad, the ship could always put into Halifax where cheap coal was available. This time the economy-conscious ship-owners gambled once too often, and the blunder cost them their ship and the lives of 481 innocent people.

Considering the immensity of the disaster, the sentences imposed by the Court of Inquiry were ridiculously lenient. Captain Williams had his master's certificate suspended for two years, mainly for neglecting to take soundings while approaching a dangerous shore at night. No action was taken against the culpable shipowners for having precipitated the tragedy by their niggardly policies.

At the time, many people felt the penalties were scandalously light. The 481 who died in the disaster would have agreed.

7

The *Louis V. Place*: Ship That Became an Iceberg (1895)

THE 735-ton, three-masted schooner *Louis V. Place* lay grounded 400 yards off the shore of Long Island. Beaten and battered by a raging winter storm that had played havoc for several days with shipping along the Atlantic coast, she was now covered with ice from the tip of her mast to her leaking hull. With the sea breaking over every inch of her deck, her crew of eight had climbed into the rigging to preserve their lives.

Rescuers on the beach, peering through a blinding snowstorm, could see the eight miserable men clinging to the port mizzenmast, but they could not reach the stricken schooner because the sea was a grinding porridge of ice that would crush a small boat like an eggshell.

Captain Slim Baker, of the Lone Hill Lifesaving Crew, squinted at the snow-shrouded schooner.

"Eight men up there in the rigging," he muttered. "How do we get the poor devils off?"

It was a good question and one that would have to be answered if any of the crew of the *Louis V. Place* were to survive.

The *Louis V. Place* left Baltimore, Maryland, on January 30, 1895, on a routine voyage—hauling 1,100 tons of coal to New York. She was under the command of Captain William Squires, a 50-year-old veteran of the seas. A crew of six sailors and a cook rounded out the ship's complement of eight. The crewmen were Soren J. Nelson, a 24-year-old sailor from Denmark; William Stevens, 30 years old with his home in Rockland, Maine; Gustave Jacoby, 44-year-old Norwegian seaman; Charles Allen, a 28-year-old sailor from Providence, Rhode Island; Fritz Oscar Ward and George Olson, both 21-year-old Swedish seamen; and Charles Morrison, a 21-year-old American cook.

No one knew it at the time, but the *Louis V. Place* was to sail into one of the worst winter storms ever to strike the eastern coast of the United States. Moving slowly against contrary winds, she had difficulty escaping the long and narrow confines of Chesapeake Bay, and it was not until February 1 that she headed northward into the open Atlantic. At that time she encountered a stiff north-northeast wind, and black clouds scudding across the sky promised a spell of unfavorable weather.

Captain Squires, taking account of the wind, shortened sail, and the *Place* spent several hazardous days and nights laboring against the wind and the growing swells of the sea. The morning of February 5 was gray and sullen, and the wind had increased to gale force. Captain Squires had all sails reefed except the foresail, and the only reason the foresail remained in place was the fact that it was stiff with ice. In fact, the entire ship was frosted with ice formed from the spray of the crashing waves.

There was a brief respite from the wind on February 6,

and the spirits of the crew brightened. The sailors managed to get the ice off the sails and hoist them again, and the *Place* made more progress that day than she had since she had left Chesapeake Bay.

Relief from the storm was short. On the frigid morning of February 7 the winds were again howling at gale force. The sails had to be reefed a second time. By this time the entire crew was cold, miserable, and tired. They had been busy combating the storm ever since they had left port, and, as a result, no one had slept for days. Some of the men already had frostbitten fingers and toes.

By 2:00 A.M. on the 8th of February the storm had become so violent that it was impossible to keep the ship on course. All the crew could do was hope that the ship would hold together and ride out the gale. Waves washed the deck with such angry fury that Captain Squires was beginning to have doubts about the ship's ability to survive. The *Place* was a floating iceberg, encrusted from her waterline to the top of her masts—in the heavy seas she was all but unmanageable.

The captain was at the wheel when one of the sailors approached him with alarm in his voice.

"There are several feet of water in the hold, sir," he said.

Captain Squires nodded. He said nothing, but he was well aware that, with her heavy coating of ice and the pounding she was taking from the sea, the *Place* could not last long. He was not even sure of the ship's exact position. He assumed he was somewhere off the coast of Long Island—which later proved to be correct—but he did not know how far off. There was no doubt in his mind that the *Place*, with water seeping into her hold, was already sinking. It was only a matter of time—a short time, perhaps —before she would go down, and there would be no hope of rescue in the raging sea around them.

There was one desperate way out, however. He could

head for the Long Island coast and deliberately ground the ship—a risky move that would either save all their lives by depositing them on shore or drown them all within a few feet of safety.

At 7:00 A.M. Captain Squires called the crew together.

"Boys," he said, "I guess we have got to go ashore and trust in a kind Providence to save our lives in this terrible gale. I've made soundings, and find we are near shore. Dress as warm as you can. Eat all you can. Drink what brandy you think you need, and when we strike, take to the rigging."

Captain Squires then set the *Place* on what he knew would be a collision course with the shores of Long Island. He and the crew stayed on the aft part of the ship as the bow pointed toward calculated calamity. A little more than half an hour later the crew heard the crashing sound of breakers against a rocky shore.

"This is it," said the captain, trying to see the shoreline through the swirling blizzard. "Remember, the rigging will be the safest place. We must try to hang on until someone on shore sees us and comes to our rescue."

A few minutes later the *Louis V. Place* struck the outer bar, which was opposite from the lifesaving station at Lone Hill. The ship reeled from the impact, then listed hard to starboard. The captain and his crew raced to the rigging, climbed up the icy masts with great effort, hoping that, if the ship settled down into deeper water, they would still be above it.

Although the crew of the *Louis V. Place* did not know it, they had already been discovered. A member of the Lone Hill Lifesaving Crew had spotted the faltering ship five minutes before she grounded. He rushed back to the lifesaving station and telephoned for help from two nearby stations—Point of Woods and Blue Point. The Lone Hill Crew, under the command of Captain Slim

Baker, was already engaged in a rescue attempt of another hapless crew. The *John B. Manning*, a four-masted schooner, had been stranded between the Lone Hill and Blue Point stations several hours earlier. A messenger was dispatched on foot through the blinding snowstorm to notify the Lone Hill crew that they had a second job confronting them when they returned from the *John B. Manning*.

The messenger reached the Lone Hill rescue squad as they were returning from a successful operation that had saved the entire *John B. Manning* crew. Captain Baker sighed wearily when he learned that a second ship had grounded and was on the brink of disaster. The crew, which had been working in near-zero weather and a blinding snowstorm for hours, were cold and exhausted, and they longed for the warmth of the station. Now, without a moment's respite, they would have to attempt a second difficult rescue. Because they were dedicated men, pledged to meet just such emergencies, they hurried immediately to the site of the second grounding.

In the meantime, the crews from the other two lifesaving stations responded to the call, and the three crews converged on the shore. The men could barely see the *Louis V. Place* as they peered through a heavy veil of driving snow, but they estimated that the ship had grounded some 400 yards from the beach. The sea was breaking with cruel fury over her decks, and the men clinging desperately to the mizzenmast rigging were in constant danger of slipping off into the sea. Three men were in the shrouds, two above them, one even higher between the crosstrees, and two on the crosstrees.

It was then that Slim Baker asked how they could get "the poor devils off."

"Might not have to," said one of the men. "They look like they're all dead up there."

"Or frozen to the mast," suggested another.

An old man with piercing eyes stared through the squally snowstorm at the ship.

"Well, now," he said, "I seen two of 'em move jest a minute ago. But the other six might be dead—or leastwise on their last legs."

The men looked at each other. They were professional lifesaving crews, but the position of the *Place* gave them an almost insurmountable problem. Huge chunks of ice along the shore crashed together and splintered in every direction as the gale swept over the water. The men knew that launching a boat under such conditions would be inviting suicide. But Captain Baker decided it had to be attempted.

Baker and four men pushed a lifeboat into the turbulent, ice-choked waters and by sheer brute strength managed to move the boat ten feet. Then a giant wave swept the boat back to shore. Wet and discouraged, the men got out of the boat.

"Bring up the Lyle gun," Baker ordered. "If we can get a line to them, we can get them off with a breeches buoy. It's the only way."

Several of the men shoved the Lyle gun through the snow, positioning it to throw a line over the ship. But before they could fire the first shot, they saw two crewmen of the *Louis V. Place* topple suddenly from the high rigging to their deaths in the icy waters below.

The crew of the *Place* had been in the rigging for several hours before the rescuers had formed on the beach. Because of their long, eight-day battle against the elements, their strength was already at low ebb, and none of them knew how long they could maintain their positions in the rigging against the numbing cold and shattering wind. Their hands and feet were frozen, their faces frost-bitten, and their clothing was covered with a thick coating of ice. They looked out longingly at the shoreline, where they could see the rescuers congregating, and they asked themselves the same question Captain Baker had voiced.

"How can they get us off?"

It was a question that plagued the minds of all eight men, and it affected each differently. Some stolidly awaited their fate, whatever it might be. Others tried to help themselves. Two sailors who showed imagination in dealing with their plight were Soren J. Nelson and William Stevens. As the wind grew colder and it became obvious that they were in for a long ordeal, Nelson said, "Unless we are taken off before night we will freeze. We have to have some kind of shelter."

That seemed impossible until they set their minds to the problem. As Stevens later explained, "We fixed some rope across from one crosstree to the other, and then wrapped the topsail around outside of the topmast rigging, so as to make a lee, and we were much better protected there than our shipmates, who had no shield between them and the wind."

The improvised windbreak helped, but not much. Stevens kept kicking his feet together to keep circulation in them, and Nelson watched him with envy.

"I wish I could do that," he said.

"Why can't you?" Stevens asked.

"My boots are full of water and frozen to my feet," was the answer.

Stevens watched his younger companion closely. Nelson was just 24 years old, with little experience in the cruel ways of the sea. He was shaking and whimpering with the cold.

Stevens edged closer to him. Nelson looked at him, and tears welled up in his eyes.

"For God's sake, save me," he cried. "I'm too young to go like this."

Stevens started striking the other man across the shoulders and back, not hard but repeatedly.

"Don't go to sleep," he admonished. "If you go to sleep, you'll never wake up. Stay alert!"

He kept pounding Nelson to prevent the young man from giving up.

The ship itself creaked and groaned at the savage onslaught of the wind and waves. Her masts swayed, and the men had to hang on with every ounce of strength they had left. It seemed only a matter of time before the masts would break and tumble into the ice-swollen sea. Stevens prayed that the rescuers on the shore would find some way to reach them before that happened

Suddenly Stevens noticed the rescue crew attempting to launch the lifeboat. He alerted Nelson.

"God bless those men," he said. "They might not get to us, but they're trying."

The entire crew of eight men breathlessly watched the boat being launched and tried to raise an encouraging cheer, but their voices were dry and cracked, as if the cold had frozen their vocal cords.

But the hopes of the men in the rigging were viciously shattered. The boat with five men in it was pushed from the shore but was immediately imbedded in the grinding ice and, when a heavy wave struck, was deposited back on shore.

Stevens glanced at Nelson. The unhappy young man seemed to give up hope. Stevens, himself, felt as if the last hope of rescue was past. But he said to Nelson, "Hang on—they'll try again."

Minutes later Stevens saw the rescuers wheeling the Lyle gun into position, and his hopes soared again.

"They're going to try to put a line aboard. I hope their aim is true."

On another part of the rigging, Captain Squires was reaching the point of complete exhaustion. He felt the strength seeping out of his arms and his body. Despite the fact that he, too, saw the Lyle gun on shore, he could hold on no longer. Completely unable to help himself, he slipped from his precarious position on the mast.

"I'm gone, boys!" he cried and then let go. His body plummeted from the mast into the sea and disappeared between the churning chunks of ice.

Horrified, Stevens and Nelson watched him fall. A shudder passed through the younger man as the captain hit the water.

"My God, the captain is gone," he muttered through half-frozen lips.

It was as if they had seen a prelude to the fate that would claim all of them. Then, before they had recovered from the blow of losing their captain, Charles Morrison, the cook, let go. There were only six men left in the rigging.

The shock of seeing the two crewmen of the *Place* fall from the mast immobilized the rescuers on shore for only a moment. Then they turned their attention back to the Lyle gun.

"They're not going to last much longer up there," said Captain Baker grimly. "This Lyle gun has to work."

The difficulty in using the Lyle gun to get a line aboard the *Place* became evident with the first shot fired. The gale was blowing with such strength that it was impossible to direct the line accurately. Although they fired it toward the mizzenmast, the wind caught the line and carried it across the topforemast. None of the men on board had the energy to descend from their perches and climb the foremast to secure the line.

The rescuers tried a second shot, but the line fell between the fore- and mainmasts. Again the crew of the *Place* could not reach it.

After two shots a snow squall interrupted the rescue attempts, completely obscuring the vessel while those on shore waited impatiently to get off another shot. When it cleared an hour later they tried a third shot. It landed across the maintopmast and again was useless to the men in the mizzen rigging.

Again the weather closed in, delaying another shot. A second attempt to launch a boat failed. Until the weather cleared enough so that the ship could be plainly seen from the shore, there was nothing more the rescue crew could do.

At this point, the rescue crew still did not know the identity of the *Louis V. Place*. There were many ships in trouble as the storm ravished a large area of the eastern coast, and it could be any one of them. Strangely, as the shore crew waited for another chance to rescue the men, a writing desk was washed ashore. The rescuers assumed it had been swept from the ship they were trying to reach, and they examined it with curiosity.

The desk contained several letters written in Swedish. The envelopes bore Swedish postmarks. One letter was addressed to a Sophernie Anderson (not on the *Place*), and another was written to Fritz Oscar Ward (a member of the *Place*'s crew). A small leather notebook contained the following address: Master Matterson, Hamilton Ferry, 106 William Street, New York. But most peculiar of all was a seaman's discharge paper found in a metal box. It was signed by F. Green, Master, and read as follows: "Name of vessel, *Von Tillson*, from Rockland, Maine, Pennsylvania to Washington, Seaman Fritz Oscar Ward.

The rescuers put all this together and decided the ship was the *Von Tillson*, and newspapers in the area displayed headlines that said:

SCHOONER VON TILLSON STRANDED
Men Clinging to Rigging

At 1:00 P.M. the weather cleared enough for the rescuers to see the ship again, and they made another attempt to get a line aboard. This shot missed the ship entirely, and at once the weather became squally again, blotting the ship from view.

It was late in the afternoon when the snow let up enough to try a fifth shot. As they prepared to make the shot, one of the rescuers pointed toward the ship.

"There are only four men in the rigging now!" he cried.

The rescuers stared in awe. Obviously, during the blinding moments of the snow squall, two more men had fallen into the sea and perished! The four who remained were motionless, either dead or near death.

They fired the shot anyway, hoping it would fall into the grasp of whomever remained alive aboard the ship. But again the line went wide of the *Place*. Two more shots were immediately attempted, but they both fell short of the four men hanging in the rigging.

Before another shot could be readied, darkness closed in, making further rescue attempts impossible until dawn.

"The night will finish them, if they haven't already died," said Baker softly. "But we must stay on hand as long as there is even a shred of hope."

They stayed on shore, huddled around a huge fire, and waited. If the weather bettered, even a little bit, they would try to launch another boat during the night. But they had no opportunity to do this. Actually, the weather worsened, the wind howling like a banshee, and the temperature dropping below zero.

The ordeal in the rigging had become a hideous nightmare. Stevens and Nelson, protected somewhat by their improvised windbreak, seemed to be the strongest of the lot, but everyone was weakening rapidly. The two men who fell during the squally weather were seamen Gustave Jacoby and Charles Allen. The four survivors watched their bodies drop into the sea, and the same thought occurred to all of them.

Who will be next?

As the Lyle gun kept missing its target and the rescue boats were unable to put to sea, the courage and morale of the remaining four seamen weakened. Why prolong the agony by holding on any longer? Why not end it all by simply letting go? In the icy waters, death would come in one cold, flashing instant, mercifully.

But the will to live was still strong, and as night closed in and their plight grew almost impossible, they vowed grimly to avoid death for as long as possible.

During the long, black night two more men died. They were Fritz Oscar Ward and George Olson. Neither fell into the sea. Ward remained frozen fast to the crosstree, hanging like a stiff rag doll. Olson slipped from the mast but was held by a rope, and he hung head-down, his body swinging grotesquely back and forth as the wind toyed playfully with it. By morning only two survivors remained—Stevens and Nelson.

As dawn broke the survivors watched with dimming eyes and diminishing strength the activity on shore. The Lyle gun was again employed, and an eighth shot was fired. The line again draped itself over the mainmast, out of reach. The ninth shot was on target, but too high. It passed tantalizingly close to the mizzenmast on which the two men held fast, but fell into the sea. A tenth shot merely fell across the deck.

By mid-afternoon Nelson was rapidly disintegrating in mind and body. He looked hopelessly at Stevens.

"I don't know . . . how we survived . . . the night," he mumbled, "but we can't make it . . . through another."

Stevens looked toward shore.

"They're trying a boat again," he said.

The rescue crew knew that the Lyle gun could not be relied on in the gale that was still sweeping the area, and as a last desperate effort they were again going to try to reach the ship by boat. Despite heroic efforts, three attempts failed as the angry sea threw the boat back on shore as if it were an empty cardboard box.

Once again night descended, and Nelson's head fell forward on his chest in resignation. Stevens, summoning all his strength, pounded him continuously across the shoulders to keep him awake.

The miracle that the rescuers and the two survivors had prayed for came at midnight. The storm had at last blown itself out. The wind slackened noticeably, the sea quieted, the tide lay at low ebb. On shore the rescuers went into action. They were not sure the two men in the rigging were still alive. They had been exposed to the raging weather for thirty-nine hours, and it was conceivable that they may have succumbed to the storm. But a successful launching of the boat represented probably the last chance to save the men.

Even though the sea had relinquished some of its fury, it was not exactly a placid lagoon when Captain Baker and six men shoved the boat into the water. The tiny lifeboat battled great chunks of ice that hammered at her hull, but the rescuers saw that they were making gains they had been unable to make before. The progress was slow, tedious, aggravating, but it was steady. As the rescuers came closer to the *Place* they could see the two men in the mizzenmast rigging by the light of a moon that was now penetrating the clouds.

"Come down! Come down! We have a boat alongside!"

To their surprise—for they were afraid the men were frozen solidly to the mast—the two seamen began to slowly descend. The sudden opportunity for rescue had given them superhuman courage and strength, and once on the deck they made their way painfully to the ship's rail at just about the time the rescue boat pulled along side. Quickly the rescuers transferred the half-frozen men to the boat and set out for shore. It was a battle to get back but they made it.

It was nearly 1:00 A.M. in the morning of February 10 when Stevens and Nelson were brought into the welcome warmth of the Lone Hill Lifesaving Station and treated for exposure. Stevens' face, neck, hands, and feet were frozen. But Nelson was worse off. His feet were frozen solid in his boots, and he was barely breathing. The lifesaving crew bathed the frozen parts of the two men's bodies in cold water and linseed oil. Stimulants were used to increase blood circulation. Then they were put to bed.

Stevens and Nelson both recovered from their ordeal. The bodies of Ward and Olson were taken from the rigging the next day. On subsequent days the bodies of all but the cook were washed ashore, adding a gruesome finish to one of the most harrowing sea experiences in history—and one of the most heroic of rescue attempts.

8

The *Veendam*:
Rescue at Sea (1898)

RESCUES at sea seem to fall generally into three categories—utter failures, partial successes, and complete successes. Of the three, the first and the last are rare. Seldom do rescue attempts fail to save anyone, and just as seldom do they succeed in saving everybody.

In the case of the sinking of the *Veendam*, though, there were no casualties whatsoever. All passengers and crewmen were saved in one of the great sea rescues of all time.

The Holland-America Line passenger steamship *Veendam*—formerly the White Star steamer *Baltic*—sailed from Rotterdam on February 3, 1898, bound for New York. Built in Belfast, Ireland by Harland and Wolff in 1871, she had been plying the waters of the Atlantic for 27 years and, despite her age, was considered a rugged, seaworthy vessel. A four-masted barkentine-rigged, iron-hulled steamer, she registered 4,036 gross tons, was 418 feet long, had a 41-foot beam, and was 31.9 feet deep. A speedy ship for her day, she could usually make the Atlantic crossing in ten days. But with the gales of winter commonplace, she required eleven or twelve days for the trip from Rotterdam to New York.

The *Veendam* was under the command of Captain G. Stenger who had climbed the nautical ladder from third officer to commander. Stenger was considered one of the most able skippers on the Atlantic run. His courage had been displayed four years earlier when he had rescued the crew of the American schooner *Mary Wells* when she was wrecked at sea. Under his command was a crew of 85, along with four saloon, five second cabin, and 118 steerage passengers. The *Veendam*'s cargo was varied and valued at almost $400,000.

Only once in her 27-year history had the *Veendam* been in serious trouble. That was in May, 1891, when her shaft broke and opened a hole in the shaft tunnel at the vessel's bottom. In this instance, however, she was able to keep the water down, and was towed safely into port by the steamship *La Flandre* from a point some 700 miles south-east of Halifax.

When the *Veendam* slipped out of the roadsteads of Rotterdam in February, 1898, that old accident had been long forgotten. Yet, in a freakish repetition seven years later, a similar mishap was about to take place.

The *Veendam* made her way through the sometimes treacherous English Channel and into the Atlantic with no trouble. On the third day out, however, gale winds swept in from the northwest, creating high west-north-west seas. The ship rolled in the swells for several hours, and many of the passengers became seasick and retired to their beds.

Shortly before 5:00 P.M. on February 6 the *Veendam*

passed through some floating wreckage in the water. Captain Stenger eyed the flotsam curiously, but since it did not seem to offer any particular problem he put it out of his mind. Then, at precisely 5:17 P.M., disaster struck.

Suddenly there was a harsh grating noise rising up from the hull of the *Veendam*, and Captain Stenger glanced quickly at his First Officer.

"We're passing over some kind of obstacle," he said.

"Aye, sir." The two words were tinged with concern.

Captain Stenger immediately contacted Chief Engineer Lichtenbolt in the engine room.

"Stop all engines!" he ordered.

Hardly had the words been spoken when there was a resounding crash. The *Veendam* rolled crazily, first to starboard, then to port. It seemed like an eternity to Captain Stenger before she righted herself, and by the time she did, the skipper already knew what had happend. The *Veendam* had struck a submerged piece of wreckage, possibly a sunken ship, and there was no telling what damage had been done to her hull. If damage was slight, the big ship, boasting seven water-tight compartments, would be able to continue. However, if the wound was of major proportions . . . the thought dangled frighteningly in Captain Stenger's mind.

It wasn't long before the report of damage reached the captain, and the news was not good. The propeller shaft of the *Veendam* had been broken, just as in her previous accident, and it had torn a monstrous hole in the bottom of the hull and destroyed two bulkheads. Realizing that water was already pouring into the ship, Captain Stenger went into action.

"Man all pumps!" was his order.

This order and others that followed were carried out with cold efficiency by the crew. All steam and hand operated pumps were set to work. While this was being done, other crew members made all the lifeboats ready for lowering in the event it was necessary to abandon ship.

"She's taking considerable water," one of the officers reported to the captain. "The three compartments abaft the engine room are flooded, and the water is now pouring through the shaft tunnel into the engine room."

The *Veendam* was sinking heavily at the stern, but Captain Stenger was confident he could keep the ship afloat for some time yet. The three forward compartments remained intact, and the water-tight bulkheads in this area were keeping the *Veendam* above water.

The passengers, especially those in steerage, were not that confident. The violence of the collision, followed by the listing of the ship, literally threw the people out of their beds. Women and men sprawled on the floor amid suitcases and other personal belongings. The air was filled with the screams of the women and the coarse voices of the men. All knew that something dreadful had happened.

As the ship righted herself the anxiety lessened, and the people began to gather their possessions and return the steerage to some semblance of order. Before this could be done, however, officers of the ship were in the steerage recruiting able-bodied men to form a bucket brigade and to help man the pumps.

"For God's sake, what's the matter?" one man asked.

"We're taking water," replied an officer shortly.

The man's jaw dropped. "Just tell me what to do," he said.

It was a matter of help or be drowned, and the passengers knew it. The men went to work diligently, following their orders as if they were crewmen, but the water came in faster than the pumps could pump it out. Before long the men knew that their efforts were in vain, and terror for themselves and their families gripped them.

Two members of the bucket brigade—Mendel Mandoff and David Devinshke, both from Kovno Guberna in Russian Poland—later described their experience.

It was after five o'clock on Sunday that there came a terrible crash. We did not know what was the matter. The women fell or sprang from their cots, forgetting their seasickness, and began to rush about shrieking in alarm. We asked to be told what the trouble was, but received no information.

The ship stopped and there began a terrible rushing about overhead. We knew that there must be some awful trouble, and we began to pray. Suddenly one of the officers appeared in the steerage and ordered all the men on deck. We obeyed and were put to work on the pumps.

Oh, how we worked those pumps! We knew that our lives depended on keeping the water down, but pump as hard as we could it was impossible to lessen the immense quantity of water that poured in.

Chala Nyitka, traveling with her father, Israel, from Sushkovalen, Kalish Guberna, Russia, gave the woman's viewpoint.

Nearly all of us were sick, and most of the women and children were in their beds when the crash came. But then our sickness was frightened away. I fainted, though, as did some of the other women. But we soon revived and ran around trying to discover what happened. When we saw the men saying the Shema [a Jewish liturgical prayer] and the children gathered about us crying, we felt as though the last moment had come.

When the men were called to man the hand pumps, the women followed them on deck. As one woman put it, "We were afraid to stay where we could not see." As the men worked on the pumps the women sat silently, praying that their efforts would keep the *Veendam* afloat.

It was not until well after midnight that a ray of hope brightened the situation. Chala Nyitka related, "We strained our eyes to see a ship, but nothing was in sight. Then there was a report and great lights shot up. Our ship was firing rockets. When we finally saw the lights of another vessel it seemed too good to be true. The rockets were sent up faster, and the lights on the other vessel grew bigger and bigger. That's when we knew they saw us."

The ship seen by the passengers and crew of the crippled *Veendam* was indeed a welcome sight. She was the American liner *St. Louis*, out of Southampton, England, on February 5, bound for New York. Under the command of Captain W. G. Randle, she had also experienced heavy west wind and northwest seas on the following day.

It was 1:22 A.M. on the morning of February 7 that the *St. Louis* first spotted the *Veendam*. As Captain Randle reported, "We sighted a steamer bearing west, half south, seven miles distant, sending up distress rockets. We bore down and stopped near her at 1:43 A.M. The captain reported her to be the *Veendam*. He asked to be taken off as the *Veendam* was sinking rapidly."

What followed was a heroic rescue in heavy seas that ranks among the most efficient and successful in the annals of sailing.

There was a full moon overhead, a fortunate circumstance since it brightened the area like a floodlight. Captain Randle calculated the distance between the *St. Louis* and the *Veendam* to be about one-quarter of a mile. There was a heavy swell on, but Randle was sure his men could reach the *Veendam* and take off her passengers. He looked at Chief Officer Thomas Segrave.

"Take a boat to her," he said, "and signal if more boats are needed."

Segrave immediately called for volunteers, and eight men stepped forward. Because of the swells and the rocking motion of the *St. Louis*, it was difficult to lower a lifeboat. Four men got into the boat and lowered away, and when it hit the water four more men slid down into it. The lifeboat rocked wildly and almost swamped as the men rowed away from the *St. Louis*. It was hard work making the distance between the two ships. Segrave described it this way.

> My men pulled to her in seven minutes. We got hold of a line. Captain Stenger was by the rail, and all the passengers were crowded about near him. He was thorough master of himself, and had his company under complete control, although there were, of course, cries of fear heard principally among the steerage people who pressed around.

After some difficulty Segrave and his eight men managed to tie up to the *Veendam*, which was now down at the stern and listing. Signals for more boats were given, and then Captain Stenger commenced to lower passengers into the waiting lifeboat. Life slings were used, and Captain Stenger personally made sure each line was properly tied before permitting the passenger to be lowered.

The first to be lowered was a baby of six months. The infant was tenderly placed in the stern of the lifeboat. Then, after five women and twenty-four children had been lowered into the lifeboat, Segrave put back to the *St. Louis* with his human cargo. Again the crew had to fight giant swells that left them on the pinnacle of a wave at one moment, and wallowing in the troughs between waves at another.

From the deck of the *St. Louis* Captain Randle squinted into the semidarkness. He could see the returning lifeboat, but he could not make out any occupants. Puzzled, he shouted to Segrave as the lifeboat drew closer.

"Why didn't you bring back any people?"

"People!" Segrave shouted. "I've got twenty-five babies aboard!"

Meanwhile, George Beckwith, Second Officer of the

St. Louis, was ordered to lower a second lifeboat. The first boat lowered was splintered against the side of the *St. Louis*, but he managed to get a second boat into the water. Beckwith and his crew battled their way to the side of the *Veendam* and tied up. This time eighteen women were lowered into the boat. Beckwith, standing precariously in the surging lifeboat, could hear the steerage passengers clamoring to be taken off. Later he reported that the cabin passengers maintained better control of themselves and allowed the steerage travelers to go first. "We will wait our turn," said one of them calmly.

The third boat from the *St. Louis*, under the command of Third Officer H. R. Campbell, picked up another eighteen passengers, most of them women, and by the time it returned to the *St. Louis*, Chief Officer Segrave was on his way back to the *Veendam*.

Most of the *Veendam*'s crew were still busy managing the pumps and could not be spared from this important task to take part in the rescue of passengers. But finally a few were assigned to lower a boat and attempt to get some of the crew to the *St. Louis* safely. Two boats were staved before they got one cleared away, and in two trips it carried fifty persons, mostly crewmen, to safety.

The three boats from the *St. Louis* did a yeoman's job. The first boat, under Segrave, took off ninety passengers in four trips over the choppy waters. The second boat, under Beckwith, rescued thirty-six in two trips, and the same number were rescued in two trips made by Campbell's third boat. The efforts of the three-boat shuttle service, plus the help of the one lowered from the *Veendam*, eventually brought all 212 passengers and crewmen safely to the deck of the *St. Louis*.

In the tradition of the sea, Captain Stenger was the last to leave the *Veendam*. Before entering Chief Officer Segrave's lifeboat, however, he had one more task to perform. He went into the main saloon and began to pile everything flammable into one huge pile—curtains, tables, chairs, and other fixtures. He then poured oil over the pile and ignited it with a match. The *Veendam* was going down anyway, and Captain Stenger wanted to make sure it did so quickly and completely. After all, his own plight had been caused by underwater wreckage of some sort, and he did not want the *Veendam* to become a semi-submerged derelict that was dangerous to navigation.

Aboard the *St. Louis* was a passenger named Aemillius Jarvis, who watched with great interest the entire rescue of the *Veendam*'s passengers and later gave a graphic description of the scene to newspaper reporters.

It was very dangerous bringing the refugees to the *St. Louis*. Almost every boat struck against the *St. Louis'* side by the force of the waves. None was damaged bad enough to be abandoned, though. The men, when they were pulled near the ship, were hauled aboard by hand, a rope having been slipped under their arms. A boatswain's chair was provided for the women. It was slow work, but haste was out of the question in that sea.

From the deck of the *St. Louis*, Captain Stenger watched the dying moments of his ship. He saw the great orange-red flames consume the *Veendam* from bow to stern as she settled deeper into the sea. Saddened by the loss of his ship, he was nevertheless gratified at the rescue of all the passengers and the crew. The transfer of all 212 passengers and crew members had been a success in spite of the darkness and the dangerous seas. It would go down in maritime history.

About ten days later Captain Randle and the crew of the *St. Louis* were honored for their work in rescuing all hands from the sinking *Veendam*. Presentations of silver cups and money were made by William H. Vandentoorn, agent for the Holland-America Line. Other awards were given by the Lifesaving Benevolent Association and the International Navigation Company. Captain Randle, in his acceptance speech, added a poignant touch to the ceremony with his closing statement.

Events are transpiring now in this country which may lead us into war, and we may be called upon to sacrifice life in defense of our country. But the satisfaction will not be as great as the saving of life, which is much more gratifying than the taking of it.

9

La Bourgogne:
Collision at Sea (1898)

A thick, unmoving fog lay over the North Atlantic, reducing visibility to less than twenty yards. It was five o'clock in the morning, and even the onset of daylight had not diminished the murky miasma through which the iron-hulled, full-rigged three-masted British bark *Cromartyshire* had been sailing for several hours. She had left Dunkirk a month before and was now sixty miles south of Sable Island off Nova Scotia on the last leg of her journey to Philadelphia, inching her way along under shortened sail at no more than five knots an hour.

Captain O. H. Henderson, standing watch with First Mate A. C. Stewart, peered through squinting eyes at the soupy haze around him.

"Worst fog I've ever seen," he said, "and I've seen a few in my time."

"Aye, that it is, sir."

"Keep sounding the foghorn," the captain advised.

The *Cromartyshire* had been sounding the horn at one minute intervals for many hours. The dismal, mourning sound of the horn was the only thing that could penetrate the dense fog that enfolded them.

Suddenly, unexpectedly, there was an answering sound—the blast of a steamer's whistle close by. Captain Henderson became rigidly alert.

"Ship off the port!" he cried.

First Mate Stewart sounded the foghorn immediately. Again the piercing whistle answered.

"It's close—damned close!" the captain warned.

The words had barely been uttered when a huge black form emerged from the fog directly off the *Cromartyshire*'s port bow. Then a tremendous crash sent the *Cromartyshire* listing violently to starboard. The log of the *Cromartyshire*, signed by Captain Henderson, described the incident in detail.

> On July 4 at 5:00 A.M., dense fog; position of ship sixty miles south of Sable Island; ship by wind on the port tack heading about W.N.W., though under reduced canvas going about four or five knots an hour. Our foghorn was being kept going regularly every minute. At that time I heard a steamer's whistle on our weather side or port beam, which seemed to be nearing fast. We blew horn and were answered by steamer's whistle, when all of a sudden she loomed through the fog on our port bow and crashed into us going at terrific speed.

(This account of the collision is open to question since a sailor named Haley, at lookout on the bow, was reported as seeing a large steamer half a ship's length *ahead* on the port bow. His account was that the *Cromartyshire* actually crashed into the steamer, just abaft the starboard bridge, opening a large hole near her engine room. There was also a report that the two ships sideswiped each other, with the steamer scraping the full length of the

Cromartyshire's port side before veering off. Both of these versions had elements of truth. An official investigation of the accident later confirmed that the *Cromartyshire* smashed bow-first into the steamer and that the two ships then scraped sides before parting.)

Continuing Captain Henderson's log:

Our foretopmast and maintopgallantmast came down, bringing with it yards and everything attached. I immediately ordered the boats out and went to examine the damage. I found that our bows were completely cut off, and the plates twisted into every conceivable shape. The other ship disappeared through the fog. However, our ship was floating on her collision bulkheads so there seemed no immediate danger of her sinking. We set to work immediately to clear the wreckage, and also to ship our starboard anchor, which was hanging over the starboard bow and in danger of punching holes in the bow. We heard a steamer blowing her whistle, and we answered with our fog horn. The steamer then threw up a rocket and fired a shot. We also threw up some rockets and fired several shots, but we neither saw nor heard anything more of the steamer.

Shortly after or about 5:30 A.M. the fog lifted somewhat, and we saw two boats pulling toward us with the French flag flying. We signalled them to come alongside, and found that their steamer was *La Bourgogne*, from New York to Le Havre, and that she had gone down. We laid to all day and received on board about 200 survivors from among the passengers and crew reported to be about 800. (These figures later proved to be excessive.) Several of the passengers were on life rafts without oars, and I called for volunteers from among my crew and the surviving French seamen to bring those rafts alongside the ship. Some of the passengers and seamen from the sunken steamer assisted us. We jettisoned some thirty tons of cargo from our forehold in order to lighten the ship. At about 3:00 P.M. another steamer hove into sight, bound westward. She proved to be the Allan liner *Grecian*, bound from Glasgow to New York.

Captain Henderson had the survivors from *La Bourgogne* transferred to the *Grecian*, and since his own ship was listing he allowed the *Grecian* to tow the *Cromartyshire* toward Halifax.

Standing on the deck, Captain Henderson tried to reconstruct the accident in his mind. Obviously the French liner *La Bourgogne* had been proceeding through the fog at seventeen or eighteen knots an hour. Just as obviously, she had been mortally wounded in the collision and had gone down within minutes. But one aspect of the accident troubled him. Only one woman was rescued and pulled aboard the *Cromartyshire*. All of the others were men.

To Captain Henderson, this fact made no sense whatever.

"Something is wrong—very wrong," he told First Mate Stewart. "There must have been foul play—that's all I can think of."

The 7,385-ton French liner *La Bourgogne* was rated as one of the finest passenger ships in the Compagnie Generale Transatlantique Line, more commonly called the French Line. She had sailed from the French Line pier in the North River, New York at 10:00 A.M. on Saturday, July 2, her destination Le Havre, France. She carried 297 steerage passengers, which included a large contingent of Italian and Austrian sailors, along with 123 second class and 83 first class travelers. The total of 503 passengers was supplemented by a crew of 222, bringing the total people aboard to 725. She also carried a cargo valued at $300,000 that included heavy machinery, coffee, dry goods, raw silk, hides, leather, bicycle parts, and assorted material.

The skipper of *La Bourgogne* was Captain Louis Deloncle, formerly captain of the *Normandie* and an employee of Compagnie Generale Transatlantique for five years. Captain Deloncle boasted a reputation as one of the most efficient skippers in the French fleet, and he had once been awarded a gold medal for bravery when the *Normandie* took fire at sea.

At five o'clock on the morning of July 4 *La Bourgogne* was traveling through a water-hugging fog at seventeen knots an hour—perhaps a little fast considering the unfavorable weather conditions. Captain Deloncle was on the bridge, peering into the thickish swirls of fog in much the same way as the skipper of the *Cromartyshire*. He did not hear the foghorn of the *Cromartyshire* until it sounded frightfully close. He at once responded with the ship's whistle, shrilling out its high-pitched warning. The two ships exchanged warnings again—and then it happened.

There was a thunderous crash, and the huge French passenger ship trembled like a wounded monster. The *Comartyshire*'s jib boom, acting like a dagger, penetrated the bridge of *La Bourgogne*. It broke through her metal plates and smashed into the engine room. Then the two ships swung together, scraping their sides for their full lengths. With the prescience of an experienced seaman, Captain Deloncle knew that his ship was fatally injured.

Only one passenger was on *La Bourgogne*'s deck when the crash occurred. He was Professor A. D. Lacasse, a language teacher from Plainfield, New Jersey, who had found it difficult to sleep that night and had ventured out on deck for a morning stroll. He, too, had heard the foghorn of the *Cromartyshire* and the answering whistles of *La Bourgogne*, but he had not attached the immediate importance to it that Captain Deloncle had. But when the two ships collided Lacasse was almost thrown off his feet, and at once he knew that this was an emergency.

Professor Lacasse's first thought was of his wife, still

apparently sleeping in their stateroom on the saloon deck. He lost no time getting to the room where he found his wife awake and wondering what had happened. She dressed hurriedly, and, at Lacasse's suggestion, they both tied on their life preservers. By the time they left their stateroom they were already aware that the big French liner was listing to starboard. On deck they found other passengers, jarred awake by the collision, crowding around the lifeboats.

Mrs. Lacasse saw Captain Deloncle on the bridge and several ship's officers giving orders to the crew to lower lifeboats. But she noticed a curious apathy had gripped the crew, as if they were paralyzed by the suddenness of the emergency that had been forced upon them. As more and more passengers emerged from the companionways and reached the deck, less and less seemed to be done to help them. As the ship began to list dangerously to starboard, excitement and then panic raced through the frightened crowd.

One reason for inactivity and confusion on the part of La Bourgogne's crew was the hopeless condition of the lifeboats. The ship had been struck on its starboard side, and the collision had destroyed several of the starboard lifeboats. The heavy list of the ship to starboard, on the other hand, made it virtually impossible—at least, highly dangerous—to lower the portside boats. But something had to be tried, and finally the crew, spurred by the danger of the moment, attempted to lower the port boats. Passengers—mainly women and children—crowded into two of the lifeboats and were gingerly lowered down the side of the ship. But the attempt proved costly. Perilously scraping the hull of the steamer as they were lowered, the two boats capsized, spilling the women and children into the sea.

This tragedy seemed to spark a violent panic. Some of

the men pushed women aside and fought with each other to get into lifeboats. One boat with forty women in it never was lowered because no one would help them. Some of the Italian sailors from the steerage drew knives, driving women and children away from the lifeboats with the pointed weapons. Later, a number of the survivors testified that they saw women stabbed to death "like sheep."

Professor and Mrs. Lacasse were having their own troubles. Seeing a lifeboat that was not entirely filled, the couple climbed into it. But moments later, when they realized there was no one to lower it, they got out and made their way toward a raft at the stern. Before they reached it, however, the big liner lurched sickeningly and listed even more to starboard. Unable to maintain their balance on the fog-slippery and slanted deck, both were swept down the declivity and into the sea. Many others went with them, shrieking in fear as they tumbled from the ship into the blackish water.

But the professor and his wife were lucky. They fought their way back to the surface of the water to find that they were not far from a life raft that had been dislodged from the ship and was floating nearby. Lacasse clambered aboard and then pulled his wife to safety.

It was from this precarious perch that Professor Lacasse and his wife saw the end of *La Bourgogne*. Only minutes after they had reached comparative safety on the raft they stared in awe as *La Bourgogne* went down. The big ship simply settled into the water like a stricken beast, lower and lower, until the final stern-first plunge. In horror they watched a huge whirlpool form around the spot where the ship had disappeared, and everyone in the vortex of the whirlpool was drawn down with the ship. Faster and faster the water whirled, sucking people, who had jumped from the ship at the last moment, down with it.

One boat of the several that had been successfully launched from *La Bourgogne* was swept into the whirlpool and capsized, tossing mostly women and children to their deaths. The victims' cries of despair and agony rang loud in the ears of the two fortunate people on the raft. The raft, luckily, had drifted just outside the edges of the giant whirlpool.

La Bourgogne was gone within forty minutes of the moment of impact with the *Cromartyshire*. Of the 725 souls aboard, 560 were lost. The 165 saved included 10 second class passengers (Professor Lacasse and his wife among them), 51 steerage passengers, 100 crew members and four subaltern officers. No first class passengers were rescued. But most remarkable of all, Mrs. Lacasse was the only woman on the entire ship who was saved!

There were many and varied accounts of what happened—or did not happen—in those terrifying forty minutes before *La Bourgogne* plunged to the bottom. Some passengers cited the crew for bravery; others charged them with ineptness. Many travelers insisted there had been a breakdown of discipline among crew members, and some charged the crew with outright cruelty.

One unmistakable hero of the disaster was *La Bourgogne*'s Second Officer Delinge. Several passengers pointed to him as "the only man who did anything for the terrified and helpless passengers." The lifeboats that were launched were lowered by him, and he was last seen standing on deck with his hand on the rigging as the ship disappeared into the waters of the Atlantic.

But, according to many passengers, the Second Officer was an exception. Christopher Brunini, for example, was among the first to charge the crew with inexcusable cruelty. He said he was unable to get into a lifeboat because the sailors kept shoving him away. Finally he

was swept into the ocean by the list of the ship and swam
for two hours before he found a capsized lifeboat. He was
unable to right it himself but managed to cling to it until
another swimmer appeared. Between the two of them
they managed to turn the boat over, and to their dismay
found seven bodies—four men and three women—
wedged into the boat. They had drowned when the boat
had tipped over.

August Pourgi told a harrowing tale. He had been deposited in the water by the list of the ship and swam for
about half an hour. Just as he felt his strength leaving him,
he saw a lifeboat floating a few feet away from him. When
he attempted to lift himself into the boat several sailors
seized him and threw him back into the water. He tried a
second time and again they tossed him back. At last he
succeeded in climbing aboard and somebody said, "Let
him be!" This time the sailors reluctantly permitted him
to stay in the boat.

But that was not all. As he silently congratulated himself on his good fortune, Pourgi saw his mother clinging
to a lifeboat only a few yards away. When she attempted
to climb into the boat one of the sailors seized an oar and
shoved her back into the ocean. As if this were not
enough, he pushed her deep into the water until she
drowned.

Charles Liebra, a French passenger returning to his
native land, was sailing with his two motherless boys,
seven and five years old. He succeeded in getting them
into a lifeboat that was about to be lowered but was
unable to enter himself because aggressive sailors drove
him away with oars. When *La Bourgogne* took its fatal
plunge, Liebra went with it, but by some miracle he rose
to the surface again and began to swim. He looked in vain
for the boat with his two boys but never found it. He
realized, then, that the boat had still been dangling on the

side of *La Bourgogne* when she went down and that his boys were lost. Heavy at heart, he felt like dying himself, but the sight of a lifeboat in the water nearby was too much to resist.

Liebra tried to board the lifeboat but a sailor struck him with an oar and assailed him savagely with boathooks. He remained in the water for eight more hours before he was finally rescued and taken aboard the *Cromartyshire*. He showed the officers of the *Cromartyshire* his bruises and cuts as evidence of the truth of the story he told.

Meholini Secondo, an Italian steerage passenger, was among those saved—but not without great effort. When he came on deck after the collision he found five men struggling with a raft. The raft was tied and chained to the deck, and there were no sailors around to help the men. All five of the men and Secondo went down with the ship, and Secondo was the only one successful in swimming away from the sinking liner. He, too, tried to get into a lifeboat and was driven off with oars and boathooks. Determined, he grasped one of the oars and pulled himself aboard. Swinging the oar savagely, he drove his tormentors off. They retreated and sat scowling at him, waiting their chance to throw him overboard. He was safe only after the *Cromartyshire* took him aboard.

Patrick McKeown, of Wilmington, Delaware, was sickened as he watched a man from Philadelphia, with whom he had become acquainted, attempting to board a raft after he had plunged into the water. But a sailor on the raft grabbed half an oar and beat him three times over the head. The American lost consciousness and sank beneath the waves.

Charles Duttweiler, a German passenger, was similarly mistreated. As the French liner went down he jumped into the sea and swam away from the ship. He was in the water about an hour when he attempted to get into a lifeboat. He was beaten off by sailors and sported a badly cut eye when he was finally picked up by a lifeboat from the *Cromartyshire*.

John Burgi had another hair-raising tale to relate. He and his aged mother had been successful in getting into one of the lifeboats that had been lowered. Apparently feeling that the lifeboat was overloaded, two sailors held Burgi while another threw his mother overboard. They watched calmly until the old woman drowned, then turned to Burgi. "You're next," one of them said, and the three sailors picked him up roughly and threw him into the water. Burgi made five attempts to get back into the boat, but the sailors beat him off with oars and tried to shove him under the boat. He remained in the water for nine hours before he, too, was picked up by a boat from the *Cromartyshire*.

Many accounts of similar brutality poured from the lips of outraged survivors. Five women, clinging to the lifeline of a boat, were near exhaustion. With malicious intent, the sailors on the boat cut the line, and the women sank into the sea. Many passengers were assaulted both on *La Bourgogne* and in the water with any heavy implement at hand. One passenger said the crew did nothing to lower lifeboats except a few they intended for themselves.

All of this added up to what looked like a sweeping condemnation of the crew of *La Bourgogne*. They were not only charged with ineptness during those precious forty minutes when rescue operations should have been handled with speed and efficiency, but they were also accused of saving themselves at the expense of the passengers and using foul and brutal methods to accomplish this.

A few days after the tragedy, S. Guard and Company, Halifax agents of the Compagnie Generale Transatlantique Line, gave their version of what happened between the time *La Bourgogne* was struck and its sinking, along with their appraisal of the crew's action in the interim.

The *Cromartyshire* struck *La Bourgogne* on the starboard side, her bowsprit coming on board just forward of the bridge, smashing No. 1 boat, then, dragging aft, damaging No. 3 and No. 5 boats, breaking in the starboard boiler hold and engine room. The whole time from the collision till she sank must have been less than forty minutes, as the purser's watch stopped at 5:50 and the collision took place about 5:10. Passengers were doubtless all below asleep at the time. Before they could get on deck the ship had taken a heavy list to starboard. The saloon passengers coming on deck would have seen all the wreckage of the collision on the starboard side, with the ship listing over to starboard, and would naturally have gone on the port side and were doubt- less standing about and in the port boats, which it was impossible to launch owing to the heavy list of the steamer to starboard. Two, we are informed, were capsized in being got into the water.

The officers' boat No. 7, on the starboard side, succeeded in pushing off when the funnel, falling, crushed it. No. 11 boat on the starboard side, it is stated, was seized by some ten or twelve foreign sailors among the passengers, who kept any one else from getting in. This boat got off and after- ward refused to come and assist the fourth engineer and other Frenchmen on a raft and pick up drowning people in the water. Of the twenty-three French sailors saved, most of them were picked up in the water. The balance probably went down with the ship when she sank, working all the boats on the port side. The men coming up from the engineers' room aft would have been in a position to avail themselves of the two or three starboard boats aft and rafts which were got into the water, as would also the third class passengers, whose accommodation was aft.

Captain Deloncle, we know, was on the bridge of the ves- sel when it went down, and no doubt, from the statement of the sailors saved, who were on watch at the time of the collision, the other officers and the rest of the sailors were endeavoring to get the port boats launched and went down with the steamer, which finally sank stern first, lying over on the starboard side, taking down the passengers and the rest of the crew.

Four days after the sinking of *La Bourgogne*, Paul Faguet, acting general agent of the Compagnie Generale Transatlantique Line, cleared the crew of the French ship of charges of ineptness.

It would be useless for me to defend the captain and subordinate officers of *La Bourgogne*. They showed themselves heroes by remaining at their posts and dying with those they could not save. Of the eighteen officers of the deck and engine departments, only three saved themselves, and then they did not leave the ship until they had done their whole duty.

Immediately after the collision officers and men alike went to the posts assigned them. Several starboard lifeboats were dashed to pieces, while the lifeboats on the port side had been rendered useless by the heavy list of the steamer to starboard. The crew, aided by some of the passengers, succeeded, however, in lowering two of them, in which women and children took their places. Unfortunately these boats had to be slipped along the hull of the steamer to be lowered and they capsized. It was only at the last minute, when all efforts were of no avail and the steamer was about to disappear that the sailors, by order of their chiefs, jumped into the sea and thirty-five of the sixty were lost.

The three lifeboats that had been launched, after having unloaded their passengers in safety on board the *Cromarty-shire*, made three more trips to pick up survivors. The firemen and coal passers were down in the engine room until the end, striving against the water which was invading it to secure the good working of the pumps. It was only five or six minutes before the steamer sank that the chief engineer, who died at his post of duty, gave at two different times two blows of his whistle, signaling the crew to cease their work of rescue and hasten away.

M. Faguet was just as emphatic in defending *La Bourgogne*'s crew from charges of cruelty. He said he could not believe for one single moment that French sailors could act in a brutal and heartless manner toward women and children.

> I am quite sure that a grievous injustice has been done in accusing the ship's crew of inhuman behavior toward the passengers. If any atrocities have been committed, they were the work of foreign sailors who were in the steerage, and comprised a variety of nationalities—principally Italian, I believe. The past records of the crews of French steamers show that they are incapable of such actions. Any number of incidents may be cited to prove that wherever it was their duty to save lives they have always acquitted themselves nobly and as sailors should.

As so often occurs after a disaster of major proportions, little could actually be proved about the actions of *La Bourgogne*'s crew under stress. Statements from panic-stricken passengers are always open to question, and the pious claims of the crew are likewise suspect. But in sifting through all the available reports on the tragedy it appears likely that the crew of the French ship did, for the most part, follow the tradition of the sea, and that if atrocities occurred they were in the main committed by foreign sailors—Austrian and Italian—who escaped the steerage and, with the know-how of sailors, took over the lifeboats and rafts for their own use.

Almost three months after the disaster, a Canadian court of inquiry announced its findings after investigating the *Cromartyshire-La Bourgogne* disaster. They failed to shed much light on the matter. The judges cleared of all blame Captain Henderson of the *Cromartyshire*, which wasn't exactly a question of prime importance anyway. But they failed completely to rule on whether *La Bourgogne*'s crew or foreign sailors were responsible for the atrocities.

Despite the fact that 560 lives were lost in the aftermath of the *Cromartyshire-La Bourgogne* collision, that most consequential question was never officially settled.

10

The Fiery Finish of
the *Volturno* (1913)

CHRISTOPHER J. Pennington, second wireless operator on the mixed freighter and passenger ship *Volturno*, was nervous and ill at ease. Several weeks before, on a crossing of the Atlantic between Rotterdam and New York, he had experienced a frightening dream. It was such a vivid and horrifying dream that the 22-year-old Pennington woke up shaking and with sweat beading his brow. He had dreamed that the *Volturno* was on fire in mid-ocean and that there was panic and chaos aboard. With the ship in flames, he had been tapping out SOS endlessly on the wireless until the heat of the fire drove him from his post.

The dream then shifted to the deck where the *Volturno* was pitching in high seas. Six rescue ships hovered around it, but because of the heavy weather they were unable to take passengers off the burning *Volturno*. In his dream he saw men and women leaping into the ocean to perish; others climbing into lifeboats that capsized in the turbulent ocean waters. When all the passengers were off the ship—some dead, some alive—the crew was permitted to leave. Pennington dreamed that he was assigned to a lifeboat that promptly smashed itself to pieces against the hull of the fire-swept *Volturno*, throwing him headlong into the water. Swimming for his life, he was eventually saved by one of the six rescue ships.

The dream had been so realistic, so terrifying, that he had written a letter to the Uranium Line asking for a transfer from the *Volturno* to another ship—any ship. But the company had refused to grant his request because he had given "insufficient reasons" for his transfer.

Now he was again on the *Volturno*, in mid-Atlantic, on his last trip across before he would voluntarily terminate his employment with the Uranium Line. And the *Volturno* was pitching in heavy seas, just as his dream had foretold. The only thing missing was fire.

The 3,600-ton steamship *Volturno*, a seven-year-old vessel of the Canadian Northern Steamship Company, and at that time chartered by the Uranium Line, slipped away from her moorings in Rotterdam on October 2, 1913, bound for Halifax and New York. She carried 564 passengers—540 in steerage and 24 in cabin class—along with a crew of 93 under the command of Captain Francis Inch. Most of the passengers were Jewish immigrants from Poland, Germany, and the Balkan countries, determined to reach a new continent and a new way of life. In her hold she carried a consignment of wines, gin, oil, chemicals, burlap sacks, rags, and other cargo—most of it flammable.

The first six days of the long journey were normal, but during the night of October 8 the wind freshened, and the *Volturno* found itself wallowing in heavy seas. Still, there was no cause for alarm. She was a stout and seaworthy ship that had met and defeated the worst the Atlantic could offer over a period of seven years. The *Volturno* had on many occasions been in more severe blows than the present one, and there was no doubt in the mind of Captain Inch but that she would run through the present difficulty with nothing more serious than a few seasick passengers and a few broken dishes in the kitchen.

What Captain Inch did not anticipate was fire—a seething, slow-burning fire that started in a forward hold and was not discovered until wisps of smoke trickled up from a forward hatch.

Captain Inch acted quickly and professionally when he saw the trail of smoke. With liquor, oil, and chemicals in the hold of the ship, he knew there was great danger that the fire would spread rapidly. He ordered Second Officer Lloyd to assemble six seamen, break open the hatch cover, and direct the fire hose into the opening.

When the hatch was pried open a heavy black smoke belched forth, and when a stream from the fire hose was directed into the hold it became even worse. Somewhere in the black bowels of the ship a violent explosion occurred, ripping the hatch open wider and throwing the seamen across the deck.

Captain Inch's plan had been to flood the forward hold and keep the ship on an even keel by trimming the after holds, but the explosion changed all that. It was now obvious, by the manner in which the *Volturno* was foundering, that the forward hold was already flooded badly, and, if the fire spread, the ship would be doomed. Either it would sink or succumb to the flames.

With its volatile cargo, there seemed no way to keep the fire from spreading, and the captain dispatched seamen to awaken all passengers and assemble them on the after deck, away from the fire. Others were assigned to clearing the lifeboats for lowering.

And in the radio room, Christopher Pennington began tapping out an SOS on the wireless. He could hardly believe what was occurring; he wondered if he was dreaming his frightful nightmare all over again or if this was the real thing.

The message went out across the churning waters of the Atlantic: "SOS steamship *Volturno* position 48:25 north latitude 34:33 west longitude fire aboard need assistance." As Pennington sat there, stunned, pecking away in Morse code, an answer came. It was from the Cunard Line's *Carmania*. She was eighty miles away and traveling at fifteen knots an hour in the heavy seas. But the *Carmania*'s Captain Barr promised to come to the rescue as rapidly as possible and increased the ship's speed to twenty knots.

By the most optimistic estimate it would take the *Carmania* four hours to reach the *Volturno*. In four hours the fire might engulf the entire ship. Pennington kept tapping away, hoping to alert a ship closer to the flaming *Volturno*.

Meanwhile the passengers, with life belts tightened, congregated on the after deck. They could see the fire forward and were dismayed at the headway it seemed to be making. The strong northwesterly wind that had come up during the night made the matter more dangerous as it fanned the blaze. From two forward holds, flames leaped as high as forty feet, engulfing the entire forward part of the ship. Raging out of control, they consumed a stack of life rafts piled at the bottom of the foremast, then licked at the wires holding the radio aerial to the mast. In minutes the wires cracked, and the *Volturno*'s transmitter went silent.

Realizing that help from other ships was the only chance they had of rescue, Second Officer Lloyd climbed the rigging in an attempt to repair the aerial. He was half-blinded by smoke and almost overcome by the intense heat, but he managed to refasten the aerial so that Pennington, in the radio room, could continue tapping out his pleas for help. Before he could descend completely the ship lurched and Lloyd was thrown to the deck. Although momentarily stunned, he managed to get to his feet and limp away from the flames at the foot of the mast.

By now Pennington was receiving replies from other vessels. Answers came from ships of six nations—the *Rappahannock* and the *Minneapolis* of the United States, the *Devonian* of England, *La Touraine* of France, the *Grosser Kurfurst* of Germany, the *Kroonland* of Belgium, and the *Czar* of Russia. All promised to rush to the scene of disaster as fast as possible. All could reach the *Volturno* within five to eight hours. But could she last that long?

Captain Inch did not really think the *Volturno* could survive even the four hours until the first rescue ship arrived. With the passengers huddled at the ship's stern and the entire forepart in flames, the captain decided to put one of the lifeboats into the water. He reasoned that even though the sea was rough, occupants of a lifeboat would be safer on the water than on the burning ship—if it could be launched.

What he did not take into account was panic. When the frightened passengers realized that the first lifeboat was to be lowered, there was a frantic rush for it. Men elbowed women aside in an attempt to climb into the boat, and Captain Inch was forced to draw a pistol to stop them.

"Women and children first!" he shouted.

One man, who had stolen an officer's jacket from a linen locker, persisted in reaching the boat. One of the crewmen stopped the attempt with a right to the jaw that dropped the man to the deck.

Finally Captain Inch succeeded in getting a boat over

the side. It was under the command of the First Officer and carried another crewman and about 24 women and children. But the *Volturno* was rolling heavily, and the seas were treacherous. No sooner had the lifeboat touched the water than it capsized. All the occupants were spilled into the sea and drowned.

Shaken by the tragedy, Captain Inch nevertheless felt that the surging sea was safer than remaining on the burning deck—which was now getting hot under his feet. He ordered another boat lowered. This one was launched safely but was soon out of sight in the churning waters. It was never located and must have capsized in the heavy swells.

Seeing that the second lifeboat had made the water successfully, Captain Inch was encouraged to lower a third. This, too, was launched safely, but its success was short lived. The boat drifted aft, and the *Volturno*'s stern, lifted high by a thirty foot wave, came down on the lifeboat, crushing everyone in it.

After this second tragedy Captain Inch abandoned his attempts to launch lifeboats and prayed that help would come to his doomed liner in time. When, just before noon, the *Carmania* hove to alongside the *Volturno*, a cheer went up from the passengers. At last a rescue ship was at hand. Now, they thought, they could be taken off the burning ship.

But the sad fact was that they could not. The *Volturno* had already lost about 100 people attempting to use the lifeboats, and Captain Barr of the *Carmania* could see the futility of trying to launch boats from his ship. Waves of twenty and thirty feet made rescue attempts impossible.

Captain Barr stood on the *Carmania*'s deck and surveyed the situation as calmly as possible. From the forepart of the *Volturno* flames leaped into the sky. The passengers and crew were assembled at the stern. There was no way to reach them. Floating a breeches buoy to the *Volturno* was impossible; it would be carried away into the violent sea. Launching boats would be a disaster. Yet, one could not stand idle and make no attempt at all. He turned to Chief Officer F. J. Gardiner.

"Do you want to try to reach that ship?" he asked.

"I'd like to try, sir," Gardiner said.

Captain Barr ordered a lifeboat lowered on the lee side of the *Carmania*, but even there the seas were so rough that the boat almost turned over. But Gardiner and several of his best oarsmen finally got the boat launched and tried desperately to cover the distance between the two ships. The task proved impossible. The courageous men in the lifeboat worked for two hours but were unable to get to the *Volturno*, and it was only with great luck that they were able to return safely to the *Carmania*.

While the captains of the two ships were trying to figure out how to approach each other and transfer the passengers, another ship arrived on the scene. She was the German ship *Grosser Kurfurst*. She arrived late in the afternoon and stood by as helplessly as the *Carmania*. One by one the ships answering the *Volturno*'s distress call hove into view—the *Seydlitz*, the *Kroonland*, the *Rappahannock*, the *Devonian*, the *Minneapolis, La Touraine*, the *Czar*—nine in all.

But the sea was so rough that work with the lifeboats was still impossible.

Since the winds were not abating, Captain Inch decided there was but one way to calm the waters enough to permit boats to be launched, and it depended on whether or not there was an oil tanker in the area. If a tanker could spill oil on the surface of the water, the viscous liquid would cut down the swells and maybe—just maybe—the passengers on the *Volturno* could be taken off in boats.

Captain Inch ordered a radio plea for such a tanker. And it was then that the *Volturno* received her first good break. In the radio room, at 6:00 P.M., Pennington heard an answer to his request. It came from the American tanker *Narragansett*, a night's distance away. Captain Charles Harwood of the tanker replied with an enthusiasm that lifted hopes.

"We'll be there with the milk in the morning!"

And that would be fine, thought Captain Inch, if the *Volturno* doesn't burn itself to cinders before that time.

As darkness fell, with the nine rescue ships still clustered around, the fiery condition of the *Volturno* was dramatically emphasized. Great orange-red flames soared upward from the bow of the ship, licked their way to the midship point, and cast a ghostly light over the passengers huddled in the stern. The *Carmania* kept her searchlight going all night, scanning the waters for any passengers who might decide to jump from the *Volturno*.

It was a weird and unbelievable situation. Here was a burning ship surrounded by nine others, and for all the help they could render, the *Volturno* might just as well be alone. No one could approach her in the surging seas. No breeches buoy could be used. The *Volturno* could go down to a watery grave in as ironic a situation as ever befell a ship at sea—with help all around it, and no help at all!

During the long tension-filled night Second Officer Lloyd, who had been injured and burned when he was tossed to the deck after repairing the radio aerial, approached Captain Inch.

"They've simply got to put boats out to save us!" he said angrily, "but none will attempt it. I want to launch a small boat and prove to them that it can navigate in these waters."

Captain Inch was wary. "I doubt that you could make it to another ship," he said.

"I think I can, sir," Lloyd replied.

Captain Inch shrugged his shoulders and told Lloyd to try it, if he wanted. Lloyd immediately corralled three seamen and lowered a small gig into the water. It was a rough battle, rowing in a dark and hostile sea under the glare of the *Carmania*'s searchlight, but in forty-five minutes Lloyd managed to reach the *Grosser Kurfurst* (the closest ship at the moment), and he and his three oarsmen were pulled up to safety.

The act inspired the captain of the *Grosser Kurfurst* and at 9:00 P.M. he ordered two boats lowered. The captain later explained what happened.

Two of the boats of the *Grosser Kurfurst* were lowered and kept at work during the whole night from nine o'clock in the evening until a quarter past three in the morning. It was almost impossible for them to approach the wreck, and the rescue of those on board the *Volturno* was possible only when they jumped overboard.

During the time the two boats were in the water, circling the *Volturno*, the sailors shouted to passengers to jump, but very few would take that chance.

The night passed slowly, and the fire pressed closer to the horrified passengers in the stern. The deck was hot beneath them, burning through the soles of their shoes and blistering their feet. There was danger that the ship's plates would buckle, and Captain Inch was not at all certain that the tanker *Narragansett*, with its precious oil, would arrive in time to remove the passengers before the *Volturno* either went down or became a mass of flames from fore to aft.

At 2:00 A.M. Captain Inch ordered Pennington to send what was to be a final message from the stricken liner. It was a cry of complete despair, aimed at all the ships around them and those who might be near.

"For God's sake, do something!"

Moments later another huge explosion ripped the *Volturno*, and the radio mast came tumbling down with a crash, ending all wireless transmission. The flames roared with renewed vigor. People screamed. The crew stood helplessly, not knowing what to do. Some of the people dropped to their knees and prayed, for now, certainly, the end was near.

But the stubborn *Volturno* remained afloat, defying the flames and the explosion. Just as a gray dawn broke over the scene, the *Narragansett* came into sight. She moved in as close as she could to the *Volturno* and began spraying her black "milk" over the sea.

That was the moment the battle turned in favor of the *Volturno*. The heavy oil reduced the swells, miraculously calming the waters around the liner. Immediately the nine rescue ships began to lower boats. Within minutes there were thirty-five boats in the water, bearing down on the *Volturno* like an invasion. The passengers, seeing real hope for the first time, responded bravely. They began jumping into the oily waters, and sailors in the lifeboats pulled them from the sea as fast as they hit the water.

On cargo nets strung over the side, the crew of the *Volturno* dangled like monkeys, handing children down from one to the other and into the boats. Elderly people, afraid to jump, descended via the cargo nets with the crew helping them.

At long last, after hours of terror, the passengers had been taken off, and then the crew followed. The last boat to leave the side of the *Volturno* carried Captain Inch, who had honored the tradition of the sea by staying with his ship until the very last. With him were some of the officers, the cook, and his dog.

Each rescue ship took a certain number of the passengers and crew aboard. The *Grosser Kurfurst* had the most, 105; the *Czar*, 102; the *Kroonland*, 90; the *Devonian*, 59; *La Touraine*, 40; the *Seydlitz*, 36; the *Minneapolis*, 30; the *Narragansett*, 29; the *Rappahannock*, 19; the *Carmania*, 11—a total of 521 out of a combined count of 657 passenge.ˆ and crew. Those who perished numbered 136.

In retrospect, the most amazing part of the *Volturno* story evolved around Christopher J. Pennington, the wireless operator, and his dreadful dream. He had dreamed that a fiery disaster would destroy the *Volturno* and it had. But that was not all. When the radio mast crashed down and transmission of messages was no longer possible, Pennington rushed to the deck. He looked wild and haggard. The horrible dream that had forced him to ask the Uranium Line to take him off the *Volturno* had come true in almost all details. The *Volturno* was ablaze in mid-ocean, just as it had been in his dream. He had tapped out messages, as the dream had foretold. He had seen passengers leaping overboard in his dream, and that too was happening.

Beside himself with anxiety and fear, Pennington took one look at the towering flames and leaped over the rail. One of the boats from the *Grosser Kurfurst* picked him up and took him safely aboard the German ship—rescuing him as he was swimming in the same way he had been rescued in his dream!

Only one thing in the dream was wrong. Nine boats had answered the *Volturno*'s distress call instead of the six he had seen in his nightmare.

But one thing was sure. Christopher Pennington had lived through the horror of the *Volturno* twice!

11

The *Eastland*:
Disaster at Dockside (1915)

Iᴛ was 6:45 in the morning of Saturday, July 24, 1915, and already a happy throng of people was converging on the Clark Street docks along the Chicago River. They were Western Electric Company employees and their families, ready to sail on five chartered lake steamers for the company's annual picnic. The steamers, chartered by the Indiana Transportation company for the outing, were scheduled to transport some 7,000 people to Michigan City and the Indiana dune country for a day of fun and relaxation.

The five steamers included the *Eastland, Petoskey, Racine, Theodore Roosevelt*, and *Maywood*, but the *Eastland* was the target ship for most of the early arrivers. Tied up just west of the Clark Street bridge, she was by far the most impressive ship of the five. A trim three-decker with towering stacks amidship, she was 265 feet long, 38 feet wide, and weighed 1,961 tons. She had seen twelve years of service on the Great Lakes and was reputed to have a speed of over 30 miles an hour, making her the fastest ship on the lakes. It was only natural that most of the picknickers—especially the children—wanted to ride on the biggest and the best.

If any of the picknickers had heard or read that the *Eastland* was unsafe, they had either forgotten it or did not believe it. The twin-screw, steel-hulled ship, built in 1903 by the Jenks Shipbuilding Company at Port Huron, Michigan, was considered at the time to be one of the finest steamers on fresh water. Despite her streamlined shape and speed, she was also judged to be one of the safest boats plying the Great Lakes.

About a year after she was built, however, her owners requested that her upper works be expanded in order to accommodate more passengers. The result of the work was disastrous. Because the *Eastland*'s hull was light, her superstructure heavy, and her general shape too narrow for her height, she became a ship plagued with instability.

It wasn't long before sailors familiar with the kind of ship required for voyages on the Great Lakes were referring to the *Eastland* as a "cranky ship." On several occasions her instability was demonstrated when she listed to port, and her frightened passengers were ordered to shift to the starboard side to correct her precarious imbalance.

At one point in the *Eastland*'s lake service, a steamboat inspector demanded that her top deck be removed and her ballast tanks remain filled at all times. The owners of the ship complied by reluctantly cutting away the top deck, but failed to enforce strictly the rule about the ballast tanks. When coming into shallower water, such as the Chicago River, the ballast tanks were often emptied.

But none of this past history bothered the excited crowd that poured aboard the *Eastland* on this sunny and innocent Saturday morning. Lugging picnic baskets aboard, they lined the starboard rail along the dock to wave good-bye to less fortunate friends, then swarmed into the elegant public rooms, and climbed the companionways to the topmost deck from which they could scan the jagged skyline of downtown Chicago. This was the day they had waited for all year, and they were going to enjoy it to the utmost.

Captain Harry Pedersen stood on the flying bridge and watched the people boarding the *Eastland*. The ship's passenger capacity was 2,500, and the captain estimated that there were now about 2,000 people aboard. It was 7:00 A.M. and time to transfer a line to the chugging tug *Kenosha* that would guide the *Eastland* out of the narrow confines of the river and into Lake Michigan.

Before supervising that routine job, however, Captain Pedersen glanced again at the boarding passengers. There were two government inspectors, under the command of Inspector R. H. McCurry, counting the passengers as they traversed the gangplank, and Pedersen knew that they would not allow the *Eastland* to be overcrowded. He was mildly concerned about the fact that the *Eastland* was listing slightly to starboard—perhaps, he thought, because most of the passengers on the ship were on that side waving to friends on the dock. He was about to order the boarding stopped when the inspectors completed their count of 2,500 and began to direct latecomers to one of the other four ships. The gangplank was then removed.

In an attempt to overcome the starboard listing of the ship, Captain Pedersen ordered the engineer to trim ship by partially filling the port ballast tanks.

"But don't overfill them," he added.

No one is certain of just what happened after the captain gave his order. Either it was misconstrued by the engineer, or the cautionary note not to overfill the tanks was not heard over the speaking tube. At any rate, the tanks were filled to the brim, and the *Eastland* straightened up, then listed slightly to port.

Meanwhile Captain Pedersen was preparing the *Eastland* to sail. The bow line was freed, and the ship, still fast to the dock by its stern line, drifted sideways into the river. At the same time deckhands made secure a hawser from the tug *Kenosha*. They were about to free the stern of the ship when the *Eastland* listed sharply to port.

Captain Pedersen felt the hairs tingle on his head. It had been a violent list, but after the sharp lurch the ship righted itself again. There seemed to be no panic among the passengers. The captain could hear a band playing on deck (they hadn't missed a note), and the happy shouts of children anticipating the boat ride to Michigan City.

Suddenly the ship shifted to port again. This time Captain Pedersen sensed the worst. There was no doubt that disaster was minutes away.

The deck was now at almost a forty-five degree slant, and the *Eastland* held this precarious position for breathless seconds. The music stopped as the musicians lost their balance and slid toward the port railing. Passengers at the starboard side grabbed the rail and held on for dear life. Hundreds of men, women, and children slid across the sloping deck, holding onto each other, grabbing at deck chairs or anything else that would give them a handhold. Members of the crew tried to drive the panic-stricken passengers to the starboard side but the incline was already too steep for them to make the climb.

Below deck there was utter confusion. Not knowing what was happening, the people fought to gain the decks, blocking the companionways as they clawed each other in their fight to reach what they thought would be a safer haven.

Then the ultimate happened. The weight of the *Eastland* as it listed to port broke the stern line. The huge ship shuddered as the line let go, and with a sickening lurch, it rolled over on its side. The *Eastland* had turned over in less than five minutes from the moment that Captain Pedersen noticed its initial listing!

When the ship went over it dumped the passengers and crew members into the dirty river water. The shrill screams of women hung in the air as the ship floated on its side, half-submerged. Children bobbed like corks in the water, then went under; some of the passengers began swimming toward the dock; others who could not swim cried in agony as the water closed over their heads. A roar of anguish went up from the thousands still on the docks and mingled with the wailing of the *Eastland*'s victims.

Those passengers who managed to cling to the starboard rail were the luckier ones. As the ship toppled over they crawled slowly onto the starboard side of the hull and held desperately to the side of the ship to await possible rescue. Those on the portside were doomed.

There were incidents of panic, of bravery, of cowardice, when and after the ship capsized. A 17-year-old girl named Alice Stejakal almost lost her life attempting to rescue three other girls. Hurled into the water when the *Eastland* fell over, she at once struck out for shore. An excellent swimmer, she grabbed one girl and took her to the dock. Then she turned and swam back to another girl and brought her in. But when she attempted to rescue a third girl, the panicky young lady fought her off and almost drowned both of them. Miss Stejakal was finally forced to let her go and just managed to reach the dock again before she collapsed from exhaustion.

Peter Vehan saw his sweetheart, Mary Kesel, swept to her death despite his efforts to save her.

> We were on the starboard side of the boat and slid to the port side when the list came. Scores of chairs and tables piled up on us and forced us apart. One chair struck Mary on the head. She was unconscious when she fell into the water. I tried my best to get to her side, but she disappeared. I searched about in the water for her, but she never came up.

When the ship first listed to port, Mrs. William Peterson, wife of a Western Electric foreman, was in her starboard stateroom. She thought at first that she was having a dizzy spell, but when the second "dizzy spell" came she was thrown to the floor of the cabin. Actually, the ship had gone over, and Mrs. Peterson realized belatedly that she was not sprawled on the floor at all but on the stateroom door.

Suddenly the door was forced open by the pressure of the water underneath. Choking and struggling as the water rose in the stateroom, Mrs. Peterson managed to fight her way to the surface. Above her head was the starboard porthole. A man climbing the starboard portion of the hull saw her through the open porthole, reached down, and pulled her to safety.

Meanwhile, in a portside cabin, only one girl out of nine managed to survive. She was Lottie Anderson, a young girl who was trying on a new dress at the time of the accident. Eight other girls were in the stateroom with her, admiring each other's dresses and speculating whether or not one of them would win a prize for the best-dressed girl. When the *Eastland* suddenly capsized, Lottie Anderson was thrown through a window into the river and finally swam to safety. She never was quite sure how she had managed to escape.

Edward Kliefgas, 11 years old, saved his mother and his

younger sister in an astonishing act of bravery and calm
courage for a young lad. The threesome was on the lower
deck when the steamer began to list. Edward, seeing the
rush of people to the normal exits, shinnied up a pole and
squeezed through a porthole, pulling himself out on the
starboard side above the water. He then asked his mother
to hand up his small sister, Mildred, and he dragged her
outside and planted her safely on the hull of the ship.
With the help of a man he also managed to get his mother
through the porthole. They were later taken off the capsized ship.

Both success and tragedy were intermingled in some
rescue attempts. Mr. and Mrs. William Thayer and their
two children, Helen, age eight, and Harry, seven, were on
deck when the ship lurched. Mrs. Thayer grabbed a
stanchion and told the children to hang onto her. But she
was unable to hold on, and she and her children were
thrown into the river. In the jumble of people falling from
the boat, Mrs. Thayer lost her husband and never saw him
again. She managed to locate her children in the water
and to tread water while she held the two children's
heads above the surface. But at last her left arm went
numb, and Helen slipped from her grasp. The boy, Harry,
was still clinging to her when a policeman swam toward
them and managed to get them ashore.

"My husband and child," she kept repeating, over and
over. But they were never found.

In another rescue attempt, William Raphael, manager
of the commission house on the dock, leaped into the
water to help two women who were in danger of drowning only ten feet from the shore. He was attempting to get
the two women ashore when a fat man, terror-stricken,
grabbed the skirt of one of the women. When he began to
drag her down with him, Raphael had to take desperate
measures. He kicked out with his feet, striking the man in

the face. But the fat man held on grimly and pulled the woman down with him. Raphael got the other woman ashore.

An unknown man, underneath the pier near the overturned ship, clung to a piling and permitted two women and three small children to climb up his body to safety. The ordeal so weakened him that he slipped into the river and disappeared.

Theodore Soderstrom and his wife were hurled into the river when the *Eastland* rolled over on its side. For a long time he held his wife, who could not swim, above the water. But two panic-stricken women suddenly tried to hold themselves up on Soderstrom's shoulder, and he lost his grip on his wife. She was pulled down by the two women, and all three drowned. Soderstrom, who was later pulled from the water, gave one of the more graphic descriptions of the moment when the ship capsized.

> The passengers were crowded on the outer rail from ten to thirty deep in places. I noticed the boat beginning to careen slightly, but at first it gave me no uneasiness. Then just before we pulled out, several hundred passengers who had been saying good-bye to persons on the dock came over to the outer [port] rail. Almost instantly the boat lurched drunkenly, righted itself, and then pitched once more.
>
> By this time passengers knew there was something wrong. But it all happened so quickly that no one knew just what to do. For a third time the boat lurched, this time slowly, and there were screams as everyone tried to get to the side of the vessel next to the dock. Many were beaten down to the deck unconscious in this mad rush. Probably a dozen persons—it might have been more—jumped into the water. But they were crushed under the side of the boat before they had a chance to swim away, for after the boat got part way over, it seemed to drop on its side like a stone.

Bertha Swanke had embarked on the picnic excursion with two other girls.

I was on the top deck with my two girl companions when we felt the ship going over. The great mass of people behind us slid toward us and literally pushed us over into the water. They fell on us and pushed us down in the water until my face seemed to touch the mud at the bottom. After what seemed to be an age I came to the top. I caught a rope and was dragged ashore. My companions were drowned.

Ross H. Geeting, a salesman who managed to climb out on the starboard hull, said the panic among the passengers was unbelievable.

The boat swung several times before the final dip. It was at that last terrible lurch that everyone at once seemed to grasp what was happening. The screaming and panic was frightful. Many women had almost all of their clothing torn off before they could get to the starboard rail to hang on or the port rail to jump. There were terrible scenes enacted around stanchions and every stable upright on the upper deck as men and women fought to get hold.

Even after the boat settled on its side there was struggling on the slippery upturned side-plates. There must have been at least fifteen or twenty of both sexes and all ages who were literally pushed off to their deaths who might have been saved if they had heeded the calls from Captain Pedersen and other ship's officers to remain quiet. I saw dozens of people drown around me, but was unable to give assistance. By a great effort I was able to climb on the upper side of the boat and managed to hold on until taken off by rescuers.

Another passenger, Lyle Goyette, had just boarded the *Eastland* when it capsized.

My wife and I had just entered the boat and were in the crowd on the main deck near the gangway. Then I heard someone shout "Get back!" and we were pushed over to one side. A moment later the boat started to list. We were all panic-stricken and could do nothing. I lifted my wife in my arms and crawled out of an opening on the upper side of the boat as it slowly went over.

The suddenness and unexpectedness of the *Eastland*'s collapse confused the crew as much as the passengers. Albert Wycoff, the chief steward, said,

> I was in the lunchroom on the main deck. I noticed the boat beginning to list. Dishes fell out of the rack and a scene of wild excitement followed. I shouted for the people to save themselves. A moment later I jumped into the water and managed to rescue three women.

Deckhand William Barrett was on the main deck at the stern when the accident occurred.

> We were ready to cast off when the boat started to list. I shouted warnings to passengers around me and tried to let go the hawser. When the boat went over I climbed to the upper side and later helped to get a number of passengers into rescue boats. It all happened in a few minutes.

Captain Pedersen may have been the most surprised of all.

> I was on the bridge and was about ready to pull out when I noticed the boat begin to list. I shouted orders to open the gangway and give the people a chance to get out. The ship continued to roll and shortly afterward the hawsers broke, and the steamer turned over on its side and was drifting toward the middle of the river. When she went over I jumped and held onto the upper side. It all happened in two minutes. The reason is a mystery to me. I have sailed the lakes eleven years and previous to that on salt water for eleven years, and this is the first serious accident I ever had. I do not know how it happened.

When the first shock of seeing the *Eastland* capsize wore off, people on the shore went into action. From both sides of the river people hurled chairs, ropes, furniture, crates, and other floatable material into the water for survivors to cling to. Every boat and tug on the river raced to the toppled *Eastland*. Docked across the river, the *Theodore Roosevelt*'s crew threw lifesavers to the people in the water.

A call went out for doctors, police, firemen, and nurses, and within minutes they were at dockside lending aid. Mercantile establishments rushed motor trucks to the scene with blankets to warm the living or cover the dead. Pullmotors and ambulances were hurried to the docks by Chicago hospitals. The telephone company strung emergency wires near the dock to aid communication. A warehouse was turned into a morgue, and the *Theodore Roosevelt* became a makeshift hospital.

A second tragedy threatened even before the first was over. People who were crossing the old Clark Street bridge to gain access to the *Theodore Roosevelt* stopped to watch the horrible sight. The rickety structure was already sagging from the weight of the crowd when policemen cleared the bridge.

There was heroic action taken by many men on the docks. One man, with a rope around his waist, swam out and rescued at least twenty-five people. He would gather two at a time under his arms and let people on the dock pull him back.

One of the shoreside heroes was policeman Henry H. Loesher who described his actions this way.

> I saw scores of men and women, many of them holding children, plunge into the water. I jumped into a rowboat [some reports say it had no oars and that he paddled it with his hands] and pulled out to the drowning. I think I got about fifty ashore. Meantime, the lifeboats and tugs hurried to the scene and picked up more than one hundred persons. I grabbed those nearest me first. At one time I had four women in the boat with me. Others I aided by dragging them from the water to the docks.

Edward Schaack, a merchant, was another hero. He was on the dock when the *Eastland* turned over. He commandeered a rowboat and paddled to midstream where he dragged F. W. Willard from the water. Noticing that Willard was a strong man and in good shape, Schaack returned to the *Eastland*, and both men climbed up on the exposed side of the ship. Between them, they helped ninety people up through the portholes onto the hull.

Every effort was being made in the meantime to rescue any persons who might be trapped inside the ship but still alive. A large force of workmen swarmed over the upper side of the hull and, with acetylene torches, electric drills, and steel saws, worked for hours cutting huge holes in the hull. Some of the men then descended into the hull searching for victims.

Although a few were still living, the rescuers found most of those trapped were dead. The rescuers inside the hull attached dead bodies to ropes, and men on the outside pulled them up through jagged holes cut in the side. Within three hours more than eighty bodies had been pulled from the wreckage.

The first and obvious explanation of the tragedy was that too many passengers had crowded the port rails as the time came for departure, but officials were not satisfied with that easy excuse. They promptly ordered the arrest of Captain Pedersen and First Mate Dell Fisher. When twenty policemen escorted the men down south Clark Street toward the city hall for questioning, a crowd estimated at more than ten thousand people nearly started a riot.

Shocked and angered by the catastrophe, and worried about loved ones aboard the ship, they needed a victim on which to unleash their wrath. The crowd surged forward in an attempt to reach the two men. One man actually approached Pedersen, striking him in the face. But the police, wielding clubs, managed to force the crowd back, and Pedersen and Fisher arrived safely at the city hall.

Rescue operations proceeded throughout the day and into the night. After dark, lamps strung by the Commonwealth Edison Company cast an eerie glow over the macabre scene. When the gruesome task was finally completed, Chicago was shocked to hear that 812 people had perished in the tragedy, with at least 22 families totally wiped out, and that hundreds more had been injured. The astounding death toll was more than had died in Chicago's Great Fire of 1871. In that catastrophe 250 had perished.

In the aftermath of the disaster, much argument as to who was responsible took place. The official inquiry gathered condemning evidence of negligence on the part of the *Eastland* owners as well as maritime officials who could have taken action before the calamity. The investigation revealed that sailors on the Great Lakes had long known about the *Eastland*'s instability, that there had been panic aboard on more than one occasion when the ship listed, that a naval architect had advised the harbormaster of the Port of Chicago that there would be a serious accident if structural defects in the ship were not remedied, and that in 1910 the owners of the *Eastland* arrogantly answered these warnings with a newspaper ad challenging any naval architect or shipbuilder to prove that the ship was not seaworthy.

The evidence made it clear that, when the *Eastland* was built, the owners were interested in only one thing—a speedy ship that could negotiate the 170-mile round trip between Grand Haven, Michigan, and Chicago twice a day. The inference was that neither the owners nor the Jenks Shipbuilding Company were particularly mindful of safety.

Besides the owners and shipbuilders, the captain and

various members of the crew came in for a share of the blame. But none of the men involved were ever proven guilty of negligence. In fact, it was not until twenty years later—on August 7, 1935—that the courts finally reached a decision on the Chicago River tragedy. It said that the owners of the steamship were not to blame, that the *Eastland* was seaworthy, and that there was no over-crowding. The blame was attached solely to an engineer who had made a mistake in filling the ballast tanks. It was a bitter decision to swallow for survivors and members of families who had lost loved ones.

What happened to the *Eastland*? The toppled vessel was raised, repaired, and sold to the government. She was put into service as a naval training ship and renamed the U.S.S. *Wilmette*. When she had served her purpose in that capacity, the ex-*Eastland* was towed up the Chicago River in 1946 and scrapped—not far from the spot where she had toppled over 31 years before in one of the most bizarre maritime accidents on record.

12

The Night the *Noronic* Burned (1949)*

I⟩T was a quarter past one in the morning, September 17, 1949. At Canada Steamship Lines' Pier Nine in Toronto harbor, the magnificent cruise ship S.S. *Noronic*—largest pleasure ship plying the waters of the Great Lakes—was snugly and comfortably moored. Her gangplank was down and her decks well lighted and, outlined sharply against the dark backdrop of night, she was a bright and impressive sight.

On the busy dock, taxicabs darted about like startled beetles, returning passengers who had been ashore for the evening. On board the *Noronic*, gay parties were in progress in some staterooms; in others, people slept fitfully, disturbed by the careless noise of the merrymakers. A few persons strolled about the brightly lighted

---

*Originally published by *Argosy* magazine, Popular Publications (Canadian Issue), April, 1960.

decks; some played cards in the sumptuous lounge; others cuddled in deck chairs in shadowy sections of the upper deck.

There was no hint of danger. Here was a ship firmly tied to the Queen's Quay, immediately available to Toronto's fire fighters, well illuminated and visible to hundreds of people on the dock and in areas adjacent to her wharfage. If ever in the annals of sailing, a ship looked completely safe and secure, the *Noronic* did.

Yet, in a linen closet on C Deck, tiny dancing flames were at that moment licking insidiously at neatly stacked piles of towels and bedding—the prelude to a fire that was to sweep the *Noronic*'s decks from bow to stern in fifteen incredible minutes, reduce her to a blackened and gutted hulk, and kill 118 of her passengers in one of the worst disasters in all of North American maritime history.

It had been a gay cruise from the beginning. Captain William Taylor, sixty-six-year-old Great Lakes veteran, who had been with the line forty-three years, felt that this gaiety was particularly fitting because it was not only the last voyage of the season, but marked the thirty-sixth year of the *Noronic*'s service on the Lakes. A small, weather-beaten man, Captain Taylor had been master of the *Noronic* for the past eight years—and he took pride in both his own record and that of his ship. On this last cruise of the summer—which was to become her last cruise for all time—the *Noronic* carried 524 passengers and 171 crew members.

The big, palatial five-deck ship, 362 feet long and weighing 6,905 tons, had begun her final voyage in Detroit, crossed Lake Erie to Cleveland, picked her way through the Welland Canal, and spanned Lake Ontario, arriving at Toronto at 6:00 P.M. on September 16. She was scheduled to continue on to Prescott, Ontario and thread her way through the picturesque Thousand Islands, but tonight she was docked in Toronto to permit her passengers to go ashore.

Fully half of the vacationers took advantage of this privilege, and had the fire broken out earlier in the evening, perhaps only a handful of persons would have perished. But the fire smoldered and sulked and waited until most shoregoers had returned, and those who had remained on the ship were either in the last throes of stateroom parties or the first throes of slumber.

At 1:25 A.M., Captain Taylor returned to the *Noronic* after spending the evening in Toronto. Walking on C Deck, he met Miss Josephine Kerr, a passenger, and accompanied her to her stateroom on C Deck, not far from the linen closet in which the fire already smoldered. He then walked forward on C Deck and up the stairs, amidship, to his own quarters on A Deck. At this time, there was no outward evidence that tragedy was in the making.

At 1:30 A.M., passenger Don Church, an insurance salesman from Silver Lake, Ohio, decided to take a walk through the C Deck corridors. On the aft part of the starboard side, Church noticed a gauze-like haze in the air. When he drew closer, he saw that blue-gray smoke was issuing from a small linen closet. Alarmed, he ran along the corridor seeking help. The only member of the crew he could find was a bellboy named Garth O'Neill, who was serving his first year on the Lakes run.

"There's a fire in a closet on C Deck!" Church shouted.

The nineteen-year-old bellboy looked uncertain. With Church trailing him, O'Neill ran to the linen closet. The closet was locked, but smoke seeped through the door cracks, filling the corridor.

"I'll get a key!" gasped O'Neill.

He disappeared for several minutes and returned with a key to the closet. Opening the door, he leaped back as flames and smoke billowed into the corridor. Frantically, he tried to put out the fire with an extinguisher, but the instrument was of little use.

"The fire hose—quick!" shouted O'Neill.

He and Church ran aft and got the hose from a hydrant. To their horror, no water flowed. By this time, the blaze was spreading into the corridor, licking hungrily at varnished surfaces and waxed floors.

Dismayed at the rapid spread of the flames, Church left and went to his family on D Deck and got them ashore without injury. O'Neill, seeing now that the fire was getting out of control, hastily punched a fire-alarm box that did nothing more than light a bulb on the bridge, then reported the blaze to a wheelsman, and woke several bellboys. He went to his room, scraped his clothing together, and left the ship. It did not occur to him to warn any of the passengers.

At 1:35, Dan Harper, a pier watchman, glanced up at the towering superstructure of the *Noronic* from his position on the dock, and his jaw dropped in horror. One of the portholes near the stern of the ship was pink with flame. He rushed at once to a phone and called the Toronto Fire Department. As he dialed the number, he looked back at the ship and saw the entire starboard side leap into a sudden flare of fire.

At 1:41, the first of eighteen fire engines arrived; but by this time, the ship was almost entirely ablaze. The failure of the bellboy, O'Neill, to report the fire at once, instead of attempting to fight it himself, had given the holocaust the chance it needed. Once it got started, there was no saving the *Noronic*.

Roaring from the open closet, the fire rushed down the waxed and varnished corridor faster than a man could run. With unbelievable speed, it crept out on deck, raced along paint-covered rails, reached out ambitiously to engulf decks above and below. Like an evil monster, not satisfied with anything less than total destruction, it cunningly blocked stairways and even the long gangplank to the dock.

Many of those who had rooms along the corridor on C Deck were either asphyxiated in their beds or trapped by the flames in the hallways. Some, awakened from sound sleep and clad only in night garments, fought their way to what they thought was the sanctuary of the decks, only to find the decks themselves aflame. Watchers on the dock saw panicky faces appear at the portholes, then fade away in a flash of crimson flame. On C Deck, bodies piled up in the corridors as people fought each other viciously to escape the fire.

All over the ship, people pushed and clawed at each other for places of advantage. But there were no such places. The entire C Deck was a mass of flames within three or four minutes after the discovery of the fire. Within ten minutes, the flames were on the decks and in staterooms. Within fifteen minutes, the entire ship was ablaze from bow to stern.

Those who managed to shove their way to the decks were faced with a hard choice. They could remain on the ship and permit the hungry flames, sometimes rising a hundred feet above deck level, to destroy them, or they could go overboard. Many felt the dark, swirling water below was preferable to certain cremation. Men and women clutched each other and jumped over the rails, screaming as they fell. Some slid down ropes and hawsers to the dock and safety. Others, risking violent death in a fall rather than face the torture of fire, leaped from the decks to the dock, breaking arms and legs and, in some cases, killing themselves. But many more, with less initiative or with fear paralyzing them, stood rooted to the deck as the flames engulfed them.

Most of the panic-stricken passengers rushed to the starboard side of the ship, which paralleled the dock, causing the giant ship to list so badly that her superstructure crashed into the pier. Through all of this, the ship's whistle kept blowing in a weird cacophony of sound that sent chills up the spines of those watching helplessly from the dock. To add to the frightening din, five separate explosions were heard as flames swept swiftly over the doomed liner.

When fire fighters arrived on the scene, just six minutes after pier watchman Dan Harper phoned in the alarm, the ship was so far gone that there was little hope of saving her. It was decided that the main task was to get as many people off the burning cruise ship as possible, and firemen scrambled up extension ladders to bring passengers down from the decks. One aerial ladder, loaded with six people, broke in two, dumping them screaming into the water.

On the port side of the ship, away from the dock, small tugs, fire boats, and water taxis came to the rescue. Ross Leich, a pilot for a harbor taxi boat, nudged his vessel against the hull of the burning *Noronic*, hoping to get some of the passengers off. To his amazement, frantic people began to jump overboard, plummeting down on his tiny boat, crashing through the roof. Some, with hair and clothing aflame, were human torches. "They just kept coming down like rain," he said afterward. "There was blood all over the boat."

There were cases of heroism and cases of cowardice. One man slid down a hawser with his wife on his shoulders. Another stood on the top deck, helping passengers down the ropes, while flames closed in on him. A doctor's assistant raced from cabin to cabin, breaking windows and helping people out. Conversely, three women threw a rope ladder over the side to the dock—then were pushed rudely aside by three men, who used it.

Captain Taylor became an immediate hero and later a scapegoat. His first knowledge of the fire came when he went to his cabin on A Deck after coming aboard the ship. As he inserted his key in the door lock, a crew member ran by, shouting, "Fire!"

Captain Taylor froze with the key in his hand. "Where?" he demanded.

"C Deck, aft!" yelled the crewman.

"Get to the pilot house and blow the siren!" Taylor ordered.

With that the captain ran to C Deck. He had just come from there, after seeing Miss Kerr to her cabin, and there had been no sign of a fire. Now he found the place an inferno. Choking on the thick smoke, Captain Taylor raced from stateroom to stateroom, pounding on doors and trying to arouse sleeping passengers. In most rooms, he received no response. He could not tell if these rooms were empty, or if the people were already overcome by smoke. Grabbing a hose nozzle, he began smashing stateroom windows to rescue those inside.

When it was impossible for him to remain any longer on C Deck, he went to the stern of the ship where he saw people attempting to slide down ropes and hawsers to the dock. Firemen were throwing up aerial ladders at this point, and Captain Taylor stood with his back to the burning deck and helped people onto the ladders and down the ropes. He could feel the heat of the flames pressing toward him from behind, but he stayed at his post almost half an hour, saving numerous lives, until at last the flames reached so close that he was forced to abandon ship. At the last moment, as the fiery tongues reached out to destroy him, he leaped over the side and was fished out of the water by rescuers.

From the dock, firemen poured tons of water into the ship, but it did little good. The fire was so hot that much of the water turned to steam as it hit the blazing decks.

Horrified firemen saw person after person burn alive at the rails.

There was tragedy on the pier, too. Stunned survivors huddled miserably on the docks like dumb animals, unable to think for themselves, until they were transported to hotels.

Like a gravely wounded monster, the smoldering hulk of the *Noronic* finally settled its stern in mud, twenty-eight feet below the water's surface. It was eight hours before the fire was brought under control and firemen could board the stricken ship. What they saw amazed even the most experienced among them. The wooden superstructure of the ship was virtually gone. Steel deck plates were buckled by the intense heat. Fire-scarred, metal lifeboats still dangled from twisted davits. The entire ship was charred and gutted.

Firemen, searching the ruins of the once-proud Queen of the Great Lakes, found cinderized bodies lying in foot-deep ashes and melted glass. One young woman clutched a small baby to her breast, but both were so badly burned that when firemen tried to move the bodies they crumbled into ashes. Other bodies were found sandwiched between scorched mattresses, and upper bunks had, in many cases, crashed down and trapped people as the flames cremated them. Dozens of couples met death in a last fierce embrace.

The enormous task of identifying the dead was complicated by the horrible condition of most of the bodies. Many could be identified only by such things as wedding rings, the unburned contents of a wallet, a child's necklace, or a melted eyeglass frame. To add to the confusion, an inaccurate passenger list was all the Canada Steamship Lines could offer, since many passengers traveled under assumed names or were aboard without being listed at all. It was December fifteenth before the job of identifying all the dead was completed. Four unidentified bodies still remain in Toronto's Mount Pleasant Cemetery. The final tabulation showed 118 passengers dead. None of the 171 crew members perished.

A special government court of inquiry was set up to investigate the fire that destroyed the $5,000,000 *Noronic*. In bitter testimony, passengers blamed the steamship line and the ship's officers for lack of leadership in the crisis. Many stated that there was no water pressure in fire hoses and that fire extinguishers were empty. They claimed, too, that fire klaxons on the ship were never sounded. Crew members blamed the passengers for yielding to complete hysteria and becoming a fear-maddened mob that they were unable to control. There were also hints of heavy drinking in some of the staterooms.

The peak of drama was reached when Captain Taylor took the stand. Under relentless questioning by government attorneys, the captain became so shaken that he could not read from a typed sheet of paper he held in his hand. After long grilling, he admitted that his typewritten list of fire-station assignments for officers and crew was eight years old, and that he had not read the printed rules of the Canada Steamship Lines that required him to post the list in a conspicuous place.

"I guess," he said, "I didn't carry out those instructions."

He confessed, under further questioning, that neither he nor the steamship company had ever given written instructions to the crew on what to do in case of a fire while the ship was docked. Neither had passengers received any instructions. As for his crew, Captain Taylor was unable to say exactly how many men were aboard when the fire started, but careful investigation eventually fixed the number at fifteen.

When it was over, a 30,000-word report condemned the owners for failure to take proper precautions against fire, since the *Noronic* lacked a sprinkler system and other fire-protection devices, and censured Captain Taylor for failure to take general charge instead of "fighting the fire as an ordinary seaman." It was determined at the investigation that there had been no continuous patrol of the ship to detect possible fires, that the crew had not been instructed as to their duties in case of fire, and that the fifteen-man skeleton crew was below the minimum needed for safety.

Although maids had been seen smoking in the linen closet during the day preceding the fire, and were suspected of having left a burning cigarette in the closet, no definite cause for the blaze was ever established. Captain Taylor, despite his on-the-scene heroism in rescuing passengers, was suspended for one year. In years since, awards totaling more than $2,000,000 have been paid to claimants.

But all this came long after the night of horror. For those who endured the fire and survived, other things will live longer in their memories. They will be sure to remember the compassion of a great city that literally threw open its doors to the victims of the *Noronic*. Toronto set up a makeshift morgue in the Horticultural Building of the Canadian National Exhibit. Injured passengers were rushed to several hospitals, and taxicab drivers offered their cabs free of charge to take uninjured survivors to hotels. Such agencies as the Canadian Red Cross, Salvation Army, St. John's Ambulance Corps, and other organizations gave aid. Clergymen of all denominations comforted the bereaved. Department stores were thrown open, and clothing and other necessities provided.

But, most of all, those who survived the *Noronic* tragedy will remember the terror of racing flames that could not be stopped, of people trapped and suffocated in smoke-filled staterooms, and of human beings turned into torches—in the most awesome and unbelievable inland ship disaster of the twentieth century.

13

The Slow Death of the
Flying Enterprise (1952)

IN the annals of navigation—from ancient times to the present—there are many examples of heroism at sea. But few can match the raw courage shown by Captain Henrik Kurt Carlsen during his harrowing thirteen days aboard the sinking American freighter *Flying Enterprise*. In a frightful storm that ravished shipping in the northeastern sector of the Atlantic during the winter of 1951–1952, Captain Carlsen's dedication to his ship created a modern-day legend that has had few counterparts in marine history.

Seafarers will long remember the hurricane force winds that swept the Atlantic in the last few days of 1951 and the early part of January 1952. The savage storm encompassed an area extending from the coast of Norway to the southern tip of Spain. All along this European coast and for several hundred miles out to sea, the towering waves endangered every ship afloat. The Norwegian tanker *Osthav* sank off the coast of Spain, the German ship *Irene Oldendorff* went down in the North Sea, and several other ships met disaster off the coast of England. Even the palatial *Queen Mary* bobbed like a helpless cork in the sixty-foot waves before she reached the sanctuary of Southampton, England—three days behind schedule.

But of all the ships that were destroyed or battered in the great storm, none died as slowly or as agonizingly as the *Flying Enterprise*. In retrospect, the reason is obvious. The *Flying Enterprise* was stubborn, and so was Captain Carlsen.

The disastrous last voyage of the *Flying Enterprise* began on December 21, 1951, when the 6,711-ton Isbrandtsen Line freighter eased out of fog-bound Hamburg bound for New York. Her cargo, worth about $2,000,000, consisted of 1,270 tons of pig iron, as well as such items as coffee, automobiles, steel pipe, and, of course, the usual mail. She carried a crew of forty men and ten passengers.

Captain Carlsen had no reason to expect that tragedy was in the offing. Although only 37 years old, he had spent 23 of his years at sea. He was embarked on his forty-fourth crossing of the Atlantic—a voyage that had become routine. Most of his seafaring experience had been gained in the Danish Merchant Marine, but after taking out American citizenship papers during World War II, he sailed as skipper of several American ships in the U.S. Merchant Marine. He was rated as an able and courageous captain, although few realized how able and courageous until the tragic voyage of the *Flying Enterprise*.

Hampered by fog, the *Flying Enterprise* gingerly negotiated the English Channel and poked her bow into the Atlantic. Almost at once she encountered rough weather caused by strong winds whipping the area. The date was December 24, Christmas Eve.

By Christmas morning the storm had worsened. The winds had reached gale force, and the *Flying Enterprise* was wallowing in heavy seas. Most of the passengers were seasick, and the automobiles, as well as other cargo, were in danger of being damaged by the wildly pitching ship. On the following day, December 26, Captain Carlsen decided there was no point in bucking the storm, which seemed to increase in violence every hour, and ordered his crew to head the ship off the wind and maintain a minimum propeller rate in an attempt to "ride out" the tempest.

During the dreadful night of December 26 the gale winds rose to hurricane force and by morning were estimated at sixty-five miles an hour. Huge waves, forty feet high, crashed against and over the rolling freighter. Captain Carlsen optimistically judged that the storm had reached its height and would at last blow itself out. Then the *Flying Enterprise* could continue her journey to New York without further mishap.

But the rough weather grew worse, and by six o'clock on the morning of December 27 it was raging with such violence that Captain Carlsen rated it as one of the worst storms he had ever encountered.

Then, at six-thirty, a monstrous wave crashed across the *Flying Enterprise*, and the freighter trembled under the savage onslaught. There was a loud cracking noise that sent a shudder through everyone on board. The *Flying Enterprise* had split open amidship! The ship's steel hull had cracked in two places!

This was a shocking and dangerous situation, but Carlsen was sure it could be temporarily remedied. Handicapped by the heavy seas and the rolling of the ship, the crew went to work repairing the damage as best they could. They lashed the ship's hull together with hawsers to prevent the cracks from widening. They filled the cracks with cement. But it was a stopgap measure. It was designed to permit them to ride out the storm, but Carlsen knew they would have to put into port for repairs as soon as the winds abated.

But the *Flying Enterprise* was not destined to put into port. Throughout the night, giant waves pounded the ship mercilessly, and when dawn came the sea appeared to be more violent than ever. Then, shortly before noon, the valiant freighter was virtually put out of commission. A great thunderous sixty-foot wave hit the starboard side of the *Flying Enterprise* with such fury that it tore the starboard lifeboat from its davits and reduced it to kindling wood. The wave ripped loose bolted-down furniture in the passenger cabins and sent the ship dangerously listing to port.

For seemingly endless seconds Carlsen, the crew, and the passengers held their breath, waiting for the freighter to right herself again. But she didn't. The cargo had shifted in the hold, and the freighter now listed permanently at an angle of about thirty degrees. Then, from the engine room, came the grim news that the engines were inoperable because lubricating oil had been lost when the ship listed.

"How long will it take to get them going again?" Carlsen asked the engineer.

"It will take hours—if we can get them going at all," was the reply.

Carlsen immediately took two important steps. He ordered his radio operator to send out a distress signal to any ships in the vicinity. Then he ordered all the passengers to don life jackets and assemble on the cabin deck. When they were all before him, he gave them the frightening news.

"Keep yourselves as warm as possible and conserve

your strength," he told them. "Rescue ships should reach us soon. When they do, it may be necessary for you to leave the ship."

Mercifully, he did not tell them *how* they might have to leave the freighter.

One, two, three hours slipped past. The engines could not be reactivated. The *Flying Enterprise* was listing more and more.

The radio operator then sent a more urgent message— the full SOS recognized by mariners as the most urgent appeal for help. Although a number of ships immediately answered the call and promised to move as quickly as possible in the direction of the doomed freighter, none of them reached the ship until nightfall. As a result, rescue attempts had to be canceled until daylight. Captain Carlsen sent the fearful passengers back to their cabins for another terrifying night.

At dawn the *Flying Enterprise* found herself surrounded by seven ships that had arrived during the night: the U.S. freighter *Southland*; the British freighters *War Hawk, Sheridan,* and *Sherborne*; the Norwegian tanker *Westfal Larsen*; the German freighter *Arion*; and the U.S. Navy transport *General A. W. Greely.*

The proximity of the seven rescue ships would have raised the hopes of those aboard—except for one thing. The *Flying Enterprise* was listing at an angle of sixty degrees! It seemed only a matter of time before she would roll over on her side and slide under the relentless waves.

Captain Carlsen made a quick and accurate appraisal of the situation that morning. The portside lifeboat was useless because of the sharp listing of the ship. The starboard lifeboat had been smashed by the huge wave that had disabled her. He looked down at the churning sea and shuddered inwardly. The *Westfal Larsen* was spraying the water with oil to quiet the waves as much as possible.

There were lifeboats in the water, but the violent winds and waves made it impossible for them to approach the *Flying Enterprise*. Therefore, there was only one conclusion to be drawn. The passengers and crew would have to jump into the sea and be picked up by the lifeboats.

"All passengers to the port rail!" Carlsen ordered.

When they had gathered along the rail he explained that the *Flying Enterprise* was in a sinking condition and that it would be necessary for them to jump into the sea and be rescued by the lifeboats. A crewman was assigned to accompany each passenger leaving the ship.

Two by two they jumped until all ten passengers and ten members of the crew were in the water. The lifeboats closed in and fished them out, but it was no easy task. In the boisterous seas a half dozen lifeboats capsized.

As soon as the passengers had abandoned ship the rest of the crew followed at Carlsen's orders. They, too, were rescued, and in the entire operation only one crewman was lost.

Captain Carlsen, however, would not budge from the *Flying Enterprise*. He elected to stay with his ship—the beginning of a modern-day sea saga that was to excite the world.

With the passengers and crew safe aboard other vessels, Captain Carlsen calmly turned his attention to his lonely existence on the battered hulk of the *Flying Enterprise*. The big freighter was little more than a useless derelict now. She had no light, no heat, no power. The heavy wave that had nearly destroyed her had knocked out the electric generators. The only means of communication he had with the ships around him was a small battery-powered voice transmitter, and he used this at once to radio his intentions.

"I will, of course, stay on board until she makes port or goes down," he said.

Although the captains of the other ships urged him to leave the freighter, Carlsen was not to be dissuaded from his position. He felt it was his duty as a captain to bring his ship to port if at all possible, and he would not listen to entreaties that he abandon her.

Not long after the rescue of the passengers and crew, Captain Carlsen received notice through the *Greely* that the Isbrandtsen Line was sending a tug to tow the *Flying Enterprise* to port. This buoyed the captain's hopes. He radioed Captain Neil Olsen of the *Greely* that, although the *Flying Enterprise* maintained a permanent sixty degree list to port she seemed in no immediate danger of sinking. He would try to get some sleep during the night, he said, and see what sort of weather—and problems— prevailed in the morning. His voice, as Captain Olsen reported afterward, was cheerful and calm.

"He really expects to sleep!" Captain Olsen marveled.

Although Captain Carlsen could not have known it, this was the beginning of a long and lonesome six-day vigil waiting for the tug from the Isbrandtsen Line to arrive. Despite his cheerful optimism that he would successfully see the *Flying Enterprise* into port, the big freighter was in dire circumstances. Her sixty degree list was increased at times to eighty degrees as she rolled in the swells. In addition, the hold was flooded, her bow under water, and her stern riding high.

Getting around in the ship was a major problem due to the weird angles and slants. Carlsen could walk nowhere, but had to crawl on hands and knees. The entire world seemed topsy-turvy to him, for he was constantly crawling on the bulkheads instead of the decks. He slept in the radio operator's cabin, on a mattress wedged into a corner of the room. He dared not close the door to the cabin for fear that he might be trapped if the ship foundered. Therefore, his bed was open to the weather, and he was cold and wet most of the time.

Food was a constant problem. On several occasions he crawled into the storage room on the main deck and salvaged some cake and cans of fruit juice. He subsisted on such meager fare until one of the ships managed to get a line across and deliver him hot coffee and sandwiches. It was like nectar from the gods.

All during those six days he was sent messages from the vessels that hovered around the crippled freighter urging him to abandon ship. There was no chance, they said, of bringing the *Flying Enterprise* into port. She was in an obvious sinking condition. It would be foolish for him to sacrifice his life—a useless gesture that would accomplish nothing.

But Carlsen refused to leave the stricken freighter. He even ignored a message from the president of the Isbrandtsen Line that he save himself. He explained, almost like a teacher to a slow-learning child, that "we captains when entrusted with a large amount of dollars' worth of cargo and mail should look after them as being our responsibility. We cannot go away and leave it." He even apologized to the captains of the ships standing by for upsetting their schedules.

Cold, wet, semi-exhausted, and half-starved, Captain Carlsen stayed with his cripped ship. The captains of the other ships admired his dedication but questioned his stubbornness. In a small village outside of Copenhagen, his mother told reporters, "My son was always a wonderful boy, but obstinate."

Obstinate he was, but he managed to ride out the storm. At last, on the night of January 3, the 4,000-horsepower British tug *Turmoil*, so aptly named for the task at hand, arrived on the scene with instructions to try to tow the mangled freighter to port.

By this time the saga of the captain who would not leave his sinking ship had been heard around the world. People all over the globe were electrified by the dramatic story.

In Great Britain the newspapers gave Carlsen complimentary nicknames, calling him Captain Enterprise and Stay-Put Carlsen. In the United States, Hal Wallis, the Hollywood producer, decided to do a motion picture called *The Flying Enterprise*. It was the reaction of a people still not recovered from World War II and weary of the new conflict in Korea; they needed a new hero with a nonmilitary background to idolize, and Captain Carlsen was ready-made for them.

It was 11:00 P.M. when the tug *Turmoil* came alongside the *Flying Enterprise*. With Carlsen standing at the stern rail with a flashlight, several attempts were made to throw a line from the tug to the freighter. But Carlsen was handicapped by the fact that he had to hold onto the railing with one hand while trying to catch the line with the other. The darkness of the night also added to the impossibility of success, and finally the attempts had to be discontinued.

It was then decided to wait until daylight, and at eight o'clock in the morning several more attempts were made. But getting the line over in the rolling sea even in daylight was a much tougher job than anyone had expected. Try after try failed. To Kenneth Dancy, mate on the *Turmoil*, it became obvious that Carlsen would never be able to catch and pull a line aboard the freighter without help.

"I'd like permission to go aboard the freighter and help him," he said to Captain Dan Parker.

"It's a risky business," said the captain dubiously.

"If we can get close enough to her, I'll try it," Dancy said.

It was mid-afternoon before the chance presented itself. The sea was still rough, and the two vessels rocked in the giant swells. Inch by cautious inch the *Turmoil* moved toward the stern of the *Flying Enterprise*. When she was only a few feet away, a giant wave caught her and bumped her against the stern of the freighter. In that split instant Dancy made his move. He caught hold of the stern rail of the rolling ship and vaulted aboard. The suddenness of the act surprised Carlsen, and he stared open-mouthed for a moment at the 27-year-old Scotsman who had made the daring leap. Dancy put out his hand, and Carlsen grabbed it.

"Welcome to the *Flying Enterprise*," he said. "Make yourself comfortable."

A feeling of elation came over Captain Carlsen at the appearance of Dancy. Later he told reporters, "It was a tremendous relief for me to have a helping hand—a companion in my loneliness."

For awhile it appeared that even two men on the disabled freighter would not be enough to secure a line for towing. More attempts were made during the late afternoon, but none succeeded. At last the two men on the slanted decks of the freighter were required to give up until the next morning. Carlsen showed Dancy how he crawled from place to place and finally took the Scotsman to the radio room where another bed was rigged up to accommodate a second person. This task finished, Carlsen climbed into his soggy bed and pulled the damp covers around him.

"Good night, Mr. Dancy," he said.

"Good night, Captain Carlsen," was the reply.

Carlsen, exhausted from the day's labor and having accustomed himself to the clammy accommodations, went to sleep at once. But Dancy did not. Later he explained why. "When a sea hit her beam-on," he said, "the whole ship would shudder from bow to stern. A dozen and one bits of gear that had broken loose clattered and scraped against the decks and bulkheads. . . . Carlsen seemed to be quite composed and able to sleep through it all."

That night the storm diminished, and the sea grew

calmer. At nine o'clock the next morning another attempt was made to secure a tow line—but this time at the bow. It had been previously thought that, since the stern was highest, it would be better to tow the *Flying Enterprise* backward. Now the two captains had changed their minds.

Evidently the new plan was the better one because before the morning was out the two men on the helpless ship had secured the line and the towing operation got underway.

Taking advantage of the lull in the storm, the *Turmoil* moved slowly and cautiously, tightening the line between the tug and the freighter. Soon the tough little tug had the freighter in tow, moving slowly through the water in the direction of Falmouth, England—300 miles away.

The next three days were encouraging not only to Carlsen and Dancy, but to the world. The storm had so moderated that the tug could tow the *Flying Enterprise* at a steady three miles an hour, and the steady progress toward Falmouth convinced the world that the gallant Captain Carlsen would at last win his battle against the elements.

Elated by the turn of events, newspapers and wire services printed everything they could about the *Flying Enterprise* and her doughty captain, as well as the bravery of Kenneth Dancy who had risked his life to board the slanted, slippery deck of the freighter. News services, broadcasting companies, and news-reel crews hired tugs and airplanes to get their own exclusive photographs of the stricken freighter and the bravely toiling tug *Turmoil*. Carlsen, surprised at all the attention coming his way, spent much of his time waving at airplanes that circled the ship.

At Falmouth, people gathered to wait for the approach of the wreck and a chance to see Captain Carlsen. A London newspaper flew Carlsen's parents from Denmark to Falmouth for the arrival. The *New York Times* reported that agents "seeking book, magazine, radio, television, and even comic strip rights" to his story were waiting patiently for the arrival of Carlsen.

But then came January 8, a black day in this strange saga of the sea.

The storm, which had run out of steam and had apparently given up in its attempt to sink the *Flying Enterprise*, suddenly renewed itself. The *Turmoil* had succeeded in towing the listing freighter to a point within eighty miles of Falmouth when the winds began to rise. Before long heavy seas were again crashing over the ill-fated ship. The little tug fought furiously against the storm's vicious encroachment, but finally was forced to heave to. For five tedious hours the *Flying Enterprise* rolled in the heavy seas, putting as much strain on the tow line as if she were being towed. It was dark by the time the *Turmoil* resumed the journey toward Falmouth. Again, as if by a miracle, the sea was calmer.

Carlsen and Dancy went to their frigid beds and attempted to sleep, but slumber came fitfully. At 3:00 A.M. now only 55 miles from Falmouth, they were roused by a frightening sound—six piercing blasts from the *Turmoil*'s siren.

"That means trouble," said Dancy.

It was trouble, indeed. The tow line had broken, and, in total darkness, it was impossible to secure another line. All that could be done was to wait for daylight again.

By the morning of January 9 the weather had worsened once more. Giant waves again washed the *Flying Enterprise*, and the tug had difficulty trying to get its stern in line with the bow of the freighter so that another line could be passed over. Before this could be accomplished, a forty-foot wave clobbered the freighter and caught both men, at the bow, by surprise. Carlsen was almost swept overboard. He slid down the slanted deck but managed to grab the port railing just as he was about to slip into the raging sea. Dancy also went head-over-heels before he managed to grab the port rail. The accident so exhausted the men that they crawled back to the radio room to rest, hoping that an improvement in the weather would make their task of getting a new tow line aboard easier.

But the weather did not improve; it grew worse. The second storm seemed hell-bent on destroying the freighter that had taken such a beating from the first one. As if guided by some malevolent hand, the waves seemed determined to finish the *Flying Enterprise* and send it to the bottom.

The gale was raging furiously as daylight came on January 10. Carlsen knew that the *Flying Enterprise* was riding lower and lower in the water. In the morning radio contact with Captain Parker of the *Turmoil*, Carlsen finally showed his first sign of conceding defeat. He said forlornly, "We can but hope and pray."

By this time the British destroyer *Willard Keith* was standing by, escorting the freighter and the tug. The captain of the *Keith* relayed an offer from the Royal Air Force to take Carlsen and Dancy off the sinking ship by helicopter. But again Carlsen turned it down.

"I'm not abandoning," he said. "The sea is playing heck with the ship, but I'm not abandoning."

Carlsen and Dancy, wanting to get as high up on the ship as possible, climbed painfully to the captain's office, the most elevated part of the listing freighter. The sixty-five degree list was increasing to eighty as the big freighter seemed on the verge of capsizing.

At 2:00 P.M. the *Flying Enterprise* was almost on its beam ends, with Captain Carlsen and Dancy still trying to ride out the storm. At this point the radio messages began to crackle between the *Keith*, the *Turmoil*, and the *Flying Enterprise*. They told the story.

2:30 P.M., *Flying Enterprise* to *Turmoil*: "Things aren't so hot here now, Captain Parker. She's taking a lot of water."

Turmoil to *Flying Enterprise*: "Your hatches are awash and may give way any time."

The two stalwart seamen rode the freighter for another half hour. Suddenly, she began to settle rapidly.

3:08 P.M., *Turmoil* to *Keith*: "The *Flying Enterprise* is going down . . . she's going down!"

3:15 P.M., *Keith* to *Turmoil*: "She is still afloat. Captain Carlsen and Mr. Dancy are now standing on the starboard side of the deckhouse. Come to windward! Come to windward! They are going to jump from the top of the funnel!"

3:19 P.M., *Keith*: "*Enterprise* now taking water down the stack."

3:22 P.M., *Turmoil*: "Captain Carlsen and Dancy have jumped! They are in the water. We are going to pull them in."

3:27 P.M., *Turmoil*: "I've got them. Both of them. They were in the water about four and a half minutes. We got Carlsen first and then Dancy."

3:28 P.M., *Keith* to *Turmoil*: "Beautiful work!"

Wet and disheveled, Captain Carlsen stood sadly on the rolling deck of the *Turmoil* and watched the *Flying Enterprise* go to its death. After almost two weeks on the stricken hulk, and only 41 miles southeast of Falmouth, he watched as the bow of the big freighter shot twenty feet into the air and then plunged into 40 fathoms of water. The sirens on the *Turmoil* and the *Keith* wailed mournfully as the freighter went down, and several sailors had tears in their eyes as they watched it.

Carlsen turned away, his voice breaking. "I did my best," he said slowly. "It could not be helped."

The drama had ended.

When the *Turmoil* arrived at Falmouth there were 10,000 people lined up on the Prince of Wales pier to welcome the courageous captain. They greeted him as a hero, cheering him as he stepped from the tug. Photographers' flashbulbs burst around him. The mayor of Falmouth made a laudatory speech, and Denmark's King Frederik IX sent his naval attaché with a message of congratulations.

After embracing his parents, Captain Carlsen faced almost 350 newsmen and quietly, modestly, told them the story of his ordeal: how he had been wet and cold for the past two weeks; how he had located some cake and tomato juice to eat and drink; how he had slept jammed between the tilted deck and the bulkhead of the radio room; how he had warmed his hands with candles; how he had read a book by candlelight when he couldn't sleep at night; how he had prayed. He described the perilous moment when he and Dancy had jumped from the ship into the swirling water, waiting until the pressure of air and water had burst open the wheelhouse door. But to describe his feelings as he stood safely on the deck of the *Turmoil* and watched his ship go down was too much for him.

"I cannot—and please do not ask me—tell you how I felt as I saw her go," he said.

Asked why he had remained aboard the freighter long after others had been safely taken off, he replied, "I thought I could take her back to port. I felt it was my duty to my owners. I am a sea captain, a seaman."

It was as simple as that.

From that time on Carlsen was beseiged by agents with offers for movie and story rights, radio and TV appearances, amounting in total to more than $84,000. The captain brushed them off. The offers astounded him, since he did not look upon himself as a hero and felt only that he had done his duty as a seaman by sticking to his ship until she went down. It was simply his job, and he had done his job the best way he knew how.

But honors were heaped upon him. Denmark presented him with the Cross of the Order of the Dannebrog, one of the country's highest civilian orders. The French government gave him the Ordre du Merite Maritime. The U.S. Senate voted unanimously to present him with the Merchant Marine Distinguished Service Medal. From all over the world he received congratulations in the form of telegrams and letters.

When at last he returned to the United States, the City of New York gave him an awesome welcome that started in the harbor with 400 ships participating, and continued with a ticker-tape parade up Broadway. The climax was a reception at which Mayor Impellitteri presented him with New York's Medal of Honor.

A lesser man than Captain Henrik Kurt Carlsen might have become pompous after such grandiose treatment, but it did not affect the captain of the *Flying Enterprise*. In fact, he showed only puzzlement at all the honors. He expressed this perplexity to Mayor Impellitteri during the reception in a way that marked the character of the man.

"Frankly," he said quietly, "I don't think I am entitled to all this. *I failed to bring my ship back into port.*"

14

The Sudden Death of the *Pamir* (1957)

THE four-masted West German bark *Pamir*, with her billowing white sails dramatically etched against the sky, made an impressive picture, for she was one of the few sailing ships still plying the seas of the world in 1957. On this particular day—early in the morning of September 21—she was slipping along effortlessly in the calm, blue-green waters of the Atlantic some 780 miles west of the Azores. She looked like a proud and autocratic queen of the past daring to intrude on a domain over which the twentieth century's larger, faster, and more modern ships held undisputed sway.

Captain Johannes Diebitsch was proud of every inch of the 360-foot, wind-propelled vessel. So were the thirty-five veteran seamen and the fifty-one teen-age cadets in training for the German merchant marine. It had been an easy, trouble-free voyage from Hamburg, Germany, to Buenos Aires, and now they were returning to their homeland. They had been at sea almost four months, and, although the trip had been a pleasant and satisfying one, the eighty-six souls aboard were now eager to return home to spend some time with their families.

But of the eighty-six men aboard the *Pamir*, eighty of them would never again see Germany. Instead, they were destined to perish because of an unexpected and freakish turn of the weather.

The 3,103-ton sailing ship *Pamir* was 52 years old when she embarked on what was to be her last voyage. She was one of the last of her kind, a survivor of the famous line of sailing ships built by Reederei F. Laeisz of Hamburg, and she was used as a commercial vessel and a training ship for aspirants to the German merchant marine. Built in 1905, she had managed to survive the ravages of two World Wars and in 1957 was still considered a stout and seaworthy ship after a half century of roaming the high seas.

The *Pamir* passed through many hands during her career. In World War I she was captured by the British. Later she became the property of the Italian Government. Then the Italians sold the *Pamir* to Gustav Erickson of Finland, who supervised a fleet of similar sailing ships. Erickson placed the *Pamir* in service as a sailing cargo ship between Finland and Australia, and for eight years she profitably carried various commodities between the two countries.

During World War II she was again taken over by the British as a war prize while lying in port at Wellington, New Zealand, and after the war ended she was returned to Erickson. He promptly sold the *Pamir* and her sister ship *Passat* to a Belgian salvage company.

Meanwhile, in Germany, the birthplace of both the

Pamir and the *Passat*, there was much agitation to get the ships back. They were sorely needed as training ships for marine officers, since one of the qualifications for such officers was that they have boyhood experience on a windjammer. Immediate negotiations were begun with the Belgian salvage company, and at last the *Pamir* and *Passat* returned to their country of origin, purchased by a Hamburg shipowner named Schlieven. His plan was to refit them and use them as combined cargo carriers and training ships.

The *Pamir* made two runs to South America for Schlieven, but when she returned from the second voyage she and the *Passat* were both impounded. Schlieven, who had spent a lot of money in purchasing and refitting the two ships, was in financial straits, and for two years the two sailing vessels were idle. In 1955 the *Pamir* Foundation was created. This foundation purchased the two ships, placed them under the management of Zersson and Company of Lubeck, Germany, and they were again put back in service.

It was on June 1, 1957, that the *Pamir* sailed from Hamburg on what was to be her last voyage. Normally she was commanded by Captain Hermann Eggers, but a family emergency made it impossible for him to go, and Captain Diebitsch was substituted. Captain Diebitsch was a 46-year veteran of the sea and rated as a highly competent skipper. He proved his standing by guiding the ship safely to Buenos Aires.

The trip across the Atlantic was enough to make the fifty-one teen-age cadets fall in love with the big windjammer, and the voyage back to Europe was calculated to increase their affection. She sailed like a sailor's dream, smoothly, quietly; tall masts reaching for the sky; white sails swelled by the wind.

But in the south Atlantic, Hurricane Carrie was

beginning to stir up a rumpus. Captain Diebitsch received a warning on September 20 that the storm was brewing and immediately calculated the probable course the hurricane would take. Normally a hurricane spawned in the south Atlantic will veer toward the west, often striking the Caribbean islands or the east coast of Florida. Captain Diebitsch decided that by steering a northeasterly course across the mid-Atlantic under a full press of sail, he would be able to outrun the hurricane and remain in safe waters.

There was nothing wrong with the captain's reckonings, except that in this case Hurricane Carrie failed to follow the expected script. Instead of veering west, she took a sharp turn east and roared into the central Atlantic, directly toward the unfortunate *Pamir*.

Actually, there was little warning that the storm was about to overwhelm the windjammer. It came up suddenly when the weather seemed balmy and calm, like a sneak attack from the rear, and the *Pamir* was in deep trouble almost before her captain, the experienced seamen, and the cadets could react.

It was eight o'clock in the morning on September 21 that it first became obvious that the *Pamir* was in for a blow. At that time the skies turned an ominous gray, and the light winds suddenly shifted and became stronger. It was the suddenness of the change that caught everyone off-guard, and minutes skidded by before the crew realized what was happening.

At shortly after eight o'clock Captain Diebitsch sounded an alarm and ordered all sails furled. Seamen and cadets scrambled into the rigging, eager to make use of their experience. Before much could be done, the sails began to rip and tear from the savage onslaught of the quickening winds. Huge waves began to attack the ship as if determined to destroy it.

Captain Diebitsch knew the *Pamir* was in mortal danger. In a matter of minutes the situation had changed. From a proud, confident ship, she had been reduced to one that groveled for mercy in the raging waters and wind that pounded her. Still the skipper felt that the *Pamir* would survive the battering. She was a rough-weather ship that had come through many storms, worse ones than this appeared to be. The captain too, had personally battled more severe blows, as had his experienced crew of thirty-five seamen. As for the fifty-one student cadets, they were among the best he had ever handled, and he was confident they would respond to an emergency with calculated efficiency.

But the winds increased in velocity, and the waves became higher and more powerful. Within two harrowing hours the *Pamir* was listing dangerously, and forty-foot waves were crashing over her deck. The winds had shredded the sails before they could be furled and the foremast had come hurtling to the deck. Then the *Pamir* took on a 40-degree list. She was now virtually on her side with the port rail under water and the deck almost vertical.

At 10:25 A.M. Captain Diebitsch ordered the radio operator to send out an SOS. The ship's position was given as 36° 56' North, 40° 20' West—which placed her about 780 miles west of the Azores. The SOS was heard by the U.S. Air Force's 57th Air Rescue Squadron at Lages Field in the Azores. The radio report said simply: "Listing at 45 degrees. In danger of sinking."

The *Pamir*'s SOS was picked up by shore stations and rebroadcast to ships at sea, and before long many rescue ships were on the way. Closest to the disaster scene was the American freighter *President Taylor*, which headed full speed for the *Pamir*, expecting to arrive during the night. Other vessels that headed for the stricken ship were the Liberian freighter *Penn Trader*, the U.S. Coast Guard cutter *Absecon*, the Canadian destroyer escort *Crusader*, the British steamer *Manchester Trader*, the British tanker *San Silvester*, the Norwegian motor tanker *Jaguar*, the Dutch tug *Swarte Zee*, the British motor ship *Hauraki*, the German motor ship *Nordsee*, and the American liner *Tacoma Star*.

At 1:30 P.M. the Coast Guard Headquarters in New York received a final message from the *Pamir*. It was a garbled report that alluded to the fact that her "foremast was smashed by the heavy sea"—and then the radio went dead.

Meanwhile, the end of the *Pamir* was approaching with appalling suddenness. The ship lay on her portside, like a monster in its death throes, and the grim crew of seamen and cadets clung to the elevated starboard railing. There was no possibility of using the six lifeboats. The three on the port side were under water; the starboard boats were so high on the vertical deck that they could not be lowered.

Captain Diebitsch knew instinctively that the great old sailing ship was in her last moments. "Get clear of the ship fast!" he cried above the roar of the storm. "Stay together! And God bless you!"

That was the finish. There was no recourse for the sailors but to leap from the canted deck and swim away from the sinking *Pamir* as quickly as possible. And this was no simple task. The men would have to swim against mountainous waves in a turbulent sea. If they were unable to do so, they would be sucked to their deaths by the whirlpool created by the sinking windjammer.

By the dozens, the men dove into the water. Each had a life preserver, but these were of only minor help against the raging ocean. Forty-foot waves came down on them with crushing force, driving them under water. Others—

stronger, luckier, or better swimmers—struck out against the savage storm and put distance between themselves and the doomed *Pamir*.

One group of fifteen men accomplished this task and, finding an oar and pieces of flotsam, managed to lash it all together with a piece of rope from a life preserver, thereby forming a makeshift and very flimsy raft to which they clung desperately. From their position they could see the *Pamir*, bottom up now, with five men clinging to the slippery hull. They had decided to take their chances with the *Pamir* remaining afloat.

Among the group of fifteen (other groups around them were fast disappearing as the sea claimed them) was a 25-year-old baker's mate named Karl Dummer who, despite his lowly occupation, was to demonstrate leadership qualities under pressure. It was he who first sighted an overturned lifeboat that had apparently broken away from the *Pamir* and was floating several hundred feet away.

"Let's go for it!" Dummer shouted. "It's our only chance!"

The fifteen men set out to reach the lifeboat. It was a tough, cruel swim that sapped their strength. They fought the great waves and heavy swells, losing sight of the lifeboat at intervals, regaining it again. The lifeboat was like a great hand reaching out to save them, but always too far away for them to grasp.

One man, tiring, lagged behind the others. A huge wave washed over him, and he never rose to the surface again. Then a second man fell behind, a third, a fourth, a fifth. Only ten of the fifteen reached the sanctuary of the lifeboat.

The boat proved something less than a true sanctuary, however. The ten weary men noticed that the stern was damaged and certainly would leak if they were able to

Although the captains of the other ships urged him to leave the freighter, Carlsen was not to be dissuaded from his position. He felt it was his duty as a captain to bring his ship to port if at all possible, and he would not listen to entreaties that he abandon her.

Not long after the rescue of the passengers and crew, Captain Carlsen received notice through the *Greely* that the Isbrandtsen Line was sending a tug to tow the *Flying Enterprise* to port. This buoyed the captain's hopes. He radioed Captain Neil Olsen of the *Greely* that, although the *Flying Enterprise* maintained a permanent sixty degree list to port she seemed in no immediate danger of sinking. He would try to get some sleep during the night, he said, and see what sort of weather—and problems—prevailed in the morning. His voice, as Captain Olsen reported afterward, was cheerful and calm.

"He really expects to sleep!" Captain Olsen marveled. Although Captain Carlsen could not have known it, this was the beginning of a long and lonesome six-day vigil waiting for the tug from the Isbrandtsen Line to arrive. Despite his cheerful optimism that he would successfully see the *Flying Enterprise* into port, the big freighter was in dire circumstances. Her sixty degree list was increased at times to eighty degrees as she rolled in the swells. In addition, the hold was flooded, her bow under water, and her stern riding high.

Getting around in the ship was a major problem due to the weird angles and slants. Carlsen could walk nowhere, but had to crawl on hands and knees. The entire world seemed topsy-turvy to him, for he was constantly crawling on the bulkheads instead of the decks. He slept in the radio operator's cabin, on a mattress wedged into a corner of the room. He dared not close the door to the cabin for fear that he might be trapped if the ship foundered. Therefore, his bed was open to the weather, and he was cold and wet most of the time.

s they tried. With all the anaged to turn the lifeboat l. Water leaked in from the would have to find means of were too exhausted. They d stay afloat until they had

re Karl Dummer, Folkert ter Schinnagel, Manfred lerich, Klaus Driebold, a whose name has escaped

rched for provisions that y found several cans of a small barrel of fresh up rockets to mark their apparently been thrown

rn whether or not they . The lifeboat was a toy plunged and careened onto the gunwales and aft. What chilled their t where the *Pamir* had othing but open water. s death beneath the

yed the spirits of the g on," he kept saying. king for us. It's only a ed up."

pitched dangerously In mid-afternoon a lifeboat, throwing all ten of the men into the sea. But they all managed to get back and set the boat right again. This time they remained afloat until darkness closed in, when the boat was overturned again. Once more the ten men righted their flimsy craft and clambered back in. This time, however, they discovered that they had lost the water barrel.

Dummer looked over his companions, studying them. He was a strong man, and he hoped the others were too.

"I don't care how thirsty we get, no salt water!" he said firmly. "Not one sip!"

The blackness of night swept over them.

At 11:00 P.M. that night the *President Taylor* arrived at the position the *Pamir* had given. A few minutes later the *Penn Trader* appeared. The two freighters circled the area, searching for either the remains of the *Pamir* or any lifeboats that might be at sea. During the night they were joined by the Canadian naval ship *Crusader* and the tanker *San Silvester*. But the darkness was so intense and the seas so heavy that they could see nothing.

When daylight came the U.S. Air Rescue Squadron in the Azores took to the skies and, along with the Coast Guard cutter *Absecon*, began to search the seas. But they, too, came up empty handed.

Slowly the truth was forced on those who searched for the *Pamir*. The picturesque windjammer had gone down with all hands. There was only a slight possibility that a few men may have reached a lifeboat and still survived.

During the long, dark, terror-filled night, the ten men in the lifeboat bailed the boat with their bare hands and talked to keep awake. They knew that if they went to sleep their relaxed bodies would be thrown into the water by a wave. But sleep kept trying to claim them, and they fought to stay alert. Then, without warning, they saw lights in the distance. It was a ship, perhaps a half mile away!

water, but the violent winds
ble for them to approach the
e, there was only one conclu-
gers and crew would have to
cked up by the lifeboats.
t rail!" Carlsen ordered.
along the rail he explained
s in a sinking condition and
r them to jump into the sea
ts. A crewman was assigned
r leaving the ship.
ntil all ten passengers and
in the water. The lifeboats
but it was no easy task. In
en lifeboats capsized.
d abandoned ship the rest
's orders. They, too, were
ration only one crewman

ould not budge from the
o stay with his ship—the
aga that was to excite the

v safe aboard other ves-
ned his attention to his
ed hulk of the *Flying*
s little more than a use-
ght, no heat, no power.
ly destroyed her had
rs. The only means of
hips around him was a
mitter, and he used this

ntil she makes port or

The ship was sweeping the water with searchlights, but the lifeboat was out of range of the fingering beams. Frantic and unthinking, two of the men decided they wanted to swim for it. Dummer stopped them.

"You'd never make it!" he shouted at them. "We can only survive if we stay together!"

The two men reluctantly admitted the wisdom of his words and collapsed in the boat, their heads in their hands. Cruelly, the searching ship moved in another direction, and the blackness of night closed in again.

The night was marked by a series of tragedies. An hour after sighting the lighted ship, Gunter Schinnagel died. Karl Dummer mumbled an awkward prayer and the men sacrificed Schinnagel's body to the mercies of the sea.

Dummer quietly took stock of himself and the remaining eight men. He decided that Manfred Holst was the worst off. The accuracy of this appraisal was proven within the hour. Suddenly Holst stood up in the boat, staggering drunkenly. Dummer knew at once what was going on in the man's mind. Holst was on the verge of giving up hope and leaping overboard.

Dummer reached out and dragged the man down. Another sailor helped to hold the struggling figure.

"It'll be daylight soon," Dummer pleaded. "Hang on a little longer."

But the man expired a few minutes later, and there were eight left in the lifeboat.

At dawn the sun rose out of the sea and brightened the watery world around them. They had drifted some distance during the storm-tossed night—how far they could not reckon. As much as they strained their eyes there was no sign of rescue ships. But at least the storm had dissipated, and the sea was calmer. They felt they had weathered the worst of the blow, and rescue was now contingent on whether or not searching ships could find them, a tiny dot on the massiveness of the Atlantic Ocean.

During that morning the eight men suffered a galling frustration. A freighter broke across the horizon, but there was no chance that they could be seen at such a great distance, and the ship disappeared on its assigned course. The dejected men slumped in their water-filled boat, wondering if they would get a break before all perished.

Dummer decided the men needed a morale booster. He opened the first can of rations. The famished group ate eagerly of the slim supply—chocolate, concentrated milk, hardtack, and a few other unpalatable basics.

All day long they floated idly, the hot sun scorching their bodies like some malevolent creature trying to drive them out of their minds. Their thirst increased, their tongues began to swell, and the misery of exposure to heat and dryness began to take a toll. Still, they dreaded the approach of night. The night would be cooler, but it would also be more terrifying. There would be no chance during the darkness for a searching ship or plane to spot them.

But the night inevitably came and with it heavier winds, and the boat again plunged and rolled dangerously in the disturbed waters. Then, about midnight, it happened again—the boat tipped upside-down for the third time. Weakened as they were, they performed a miracle by righting the boat and climbing aboard.

But the capsizing of the boat took its toll. A few minutes later the seaman named Meine began to chatter and rave maniacally.

"He must have swallowed salt water when we tipped over," reasoned Dummer. "He's out of his head!"

Meine proved it when he suddenly leaped to his feet and shouted, "I've got to see the captain!" Before anyone could stop him, he leaped into the sea.

There were now seven men still afloat.

Before the long night was over, death claimed still

another man. Peter Frederich, losing all reason, muttered something that sounded like, "I'm going below for my sweater—it's cold." Then he plunged into the water. Once in the water, though, he must have realized his peril, for he screamed crazily. But he could not make it back to the boat, and he disappeared.

Six were now left.

What happens to men exposed to the sea for long periods with little food and no water occurred to the six men in the *Pamir*'s lifeboat as morning broke. Each began to suffer hallucinations. They saw land ahead of them. They saw rocky coasts. They even saw cities. But there was nothing.

Dummer, still the most rational of all the suffering men in the lifeboat, recognized the symptoms and decided to put the men to work at some simple task to occupy their minds. He found a couple of oil skins and a loose board and put the crewmen to work raising a sail. There were a few brief moments of activity and then the sail was in place. The men fell back into the boat, knowing in their hearts that the makeshift sail would do little good. Most of them dozed.

While five men slept, a sixth calmly got out of the boat and began to swim along with it. One of the men awakened and, seeing him in the water, shouted, "Get back in the boat! There are sharks around!"

"Don't worry, I'm all right," said the man. It was Klaus Driebold.

The awakened man, unable to keep his eyes open, dozed off again. When he awakened toward the end of the day, Driebold was gone.

Five men remained.

They drifted lazily. The men were now succumbing to the rigors of their ordeal. They lay in the bottom of the leaky boat, oblivious to their wetness, sleeping, almost dead. In their semi-consciousness, they heard someone say, "A ship! A ship!" They reacted with surprising alertness, eyes opening, clawing at the gunwales of the boat, peering into the distance.

As if by magic, a ship had loomed on the horizon. At first Dummer, who had seemed to retain most of his senses, thought it was another hallucination. But as the ship grew larger and larger he knew at last that a rescue ship had spotted them.

"It's coming toward us!" he cried.

The weakened men struggled to their feet, waving their arms frantically. Finally the ship approached close enough for the men to see sailors on the deck, waving back to them. Then they saw the name on the bow, *Saxon*.

Boats were lowered and the five men were transferred to the *Saxon*. She was an American freighter out of New York.

In the ship's hospital the men received medication, food, and drink. A few hours later they were transferred to the U.S. Navy Transport *Geiger*. The *Geiger* took them to nearby Casablanca from which they were later flown to their homes in Germany.

But the search for survivors was not over. The next day another man was found by the U.S. Coast Guard cutter *Absecon*. He was Gunter Hasselbach. He was found sitting in a lifeboat about 600 miles off the Azores. He told a tragic story. The lifeboat had held 25 men from the *Pamir*. During the first night afloat, the lights of a great steamer loomed close to them. Twenty-four of the men decided to swim toward the ship. But the ship's crew did not see the men in the water and steamed away. As Hasselbach watched in horror the twenty-four men drowned one by one in the crashing waves around them.

For nine more days the U.S. Air Force scanned the

waters for possible survivors. They spotted debris where the *Pamir* had gone down, but no more men.

Hurricane Carrie had destroyed one of the world's last remaining windjammers and in the process had claimed the lives of eighty young men, capriciously allowing six to live.

15

The *Carl D. Bradley*: A Visit to Hell (1958)

ON the Great Lakes, November is one of the cruelest and most vicious months of the year. It is the time when Great Lakes freighters are making their final trips before winter storms move in to put an end to the shipping season. Usually the freighters make this perilous last journey without incident, returning to home ports where they rest until Coast Guard icebreakers carve a new passage for them in the spring. But sometimes an early winter storm hits unexpectedly—and the result is often disastrous. So it was for a magnificent freighter called the *Carl D. Bradley*.

It was November 18, 1958. The 639-foot limestone carrier *Carl D. Bradley*—owned by the Bradley Transportation Line, a division of the U.S. Steel Corporation—had just completed a trip from Rogers City on Michigan's Lake Huron coast, through the Straits of

Mackinac, and down the banana-shaped length of Lake Michigan to Buffington, Indiana, where she had deposited her cargo of limestone. Now, on her return trip, she was nearing the Beaver Island archipelago in the upper part of Lake Michigan, headed for a winter rest at Rogers City.

She had earned the rest. The *Bradley* was completing her 46th trip of the 1958 season and had already traveled 27,000 miles in good weather and bad. Although she was 31 years old, the *Bradley* was a stout, strong ship with years of service still ahead of her. And she enjoyed a distinguished service record that marked her as one of the finest cargo carriers ever to ply the waters of the Great Lakes.

Built in 1927 at Lorain, Ohio, the *Bradley* entered service as the longest freighter sailing the inland seas. With her 639-foot steel hull, she was judged to be virtually unsinkable and one of the safest freighters then in service. Her mettle was tested two years after she was launched when she set a record by carrying the largest single cargo—18,114 tons of limestone—ever transported on the Lakes. In 1958, when she made her ill-fated last voyage, she was still one of the monster ships in service, even though a few carriers built later were close to 700 feet long.

Skipper of the *Bradley* was Captain Roland Bryan, who had taken the job in 1954. He had become a sailor at the age of fourteen, had spent seventeen years as mate and seven more as a captain in the Bradley Transportation Line before being named skipper of the *Bradley*. Serving under him was a crew of thirty-five.

It is interesting to note that two weeks before the *Bradley*'s final trip, she had ruptured a plate when she scraped bottom at Cedarville, Michigan. But solid repairs had been made, and the ship was pronounced seaworthy.

The *Bradley* was the number two ship in the Bradley Transportation Line fleet that, a few months earlier, was lauded by the National Safety Council as the safest in the world.

It was not exactly perfect sailing weather when the *Bradley* left the dock at Buffington, Indiana, at 6:30 P.M. on November 17, heading north into Lake Michigan. Waves, whipped by a persistent wind, were expected to add some difficulty to the voyage home, but no one expected any serious trouble. The worst that could happen would be a slight delay in making port.

But that night the southwest winds increased in velocity, and the waves became more mountainous, pounding the *Bradley* and breaking over her bow. By the next morning—November 18—gale warnings were up on Lake Michigan, and smaller craft headed for the security of the nearest ports.

Still there was no real cause for alarm. Captain Bryan considered all the factors involved and could not see why the big ship could not ride out the storm. She had been doing just that for 31 years, and this was a minor blow compared to some she had successfully weathered.

It looked as if she would weather this one too, for by late afternoon she was approaching the northern limits of Lake Michigan near the Beaver Island archipelago and would soon enter the more protected waters of the Straits of Mackinac.

At 5:15 P.M., with the ship taking the storm like a true veteran, Captain Bryan radioed the Bradley Transportation Line that he would be bringing his ship into Rogers City by 2:00 A.M. Little did he know that within sixteen minutes the *Bradley* would be in mortal danger, and within half an hour would plunge to the bottom of the storm-tossed lake.

Captain Bryan and first mate Elmer Fleming were both on watch in the pilot house when the first indication of danger came. Darkness was already approaching. Towering waves had been pounding the *Bradley* for hours, but the gallant ship was shrugging them off like a clever boxer fending off blows. Then, at 5:31 P.M., the *Bradley* was hit simultaneously, fore and aft, by two great waves. At the moment of impact there was an ominous thud, like some cosmic hammer striking a blow at the ship. Captain Bryan and Fleming spun around and looked down the length of the ship toward the stern. To their horror they saw that the aft section of the long ship was sagging.

That meant only one thing to Captain Bryan. The *Bradley* was breaking up. Acting quickly, he halted the engines and sounded a general alarm. Moments later a second thunking noise occurred; the ship raised in the center, settled back, and the aft section sagged even more.

"We're breaking in two," said Captain Bryan grimly. "Send out distress signals—quick!"

Fleming grabbed the radio phone and shouted at the top of his voice.

"Mayday! Mayday! Mayday!"

This was the distress signal familiar to any skipper who sailed the Great Lakes. It was a corruption of the cry that came from French explorers and voyageurs three hundred years ago—*M'aidez! M'aidez!*

Down in the conveyer room watchman Frank Mayes heard the first thunking noise, then the general alarm, followed by the second thud. Alarmed, he started for a companionway leading to the deck.

Meantime, first mate Fleming was speaking rapidly into the radio phone, pleading for help from any ship that might be nearby.

"This is the *Carl D. Bradley*. Position twelve miles southwest of Gull Island. We are in trouble. Mayday! Mayday! Mayday!"

At the same time that Fleming was pleading for help,

Captain Bryan was shouting orders to his crew. The skipper's voice went out over the air and was heard by many startled short-wave radio operators.

"Get your life jackets! Run and get your life jackets!"

Then came the third thump, and the aft section looked as if it had broken completely away from the rest of the ship. Fleming kept talking into the radio phone. Again he gave the ship's position, and then in a frantic voice, "We're breaking up! We're going to go down! Mayday! Mayday!"

Captain Bryan, knowing now that his ship was doomed, gave seven blasts on the whistle, followed by one long one. It was the signal to abandon ship.

The fourth thump finished the *Bradley*. The ship humped in the middle, settled back, and then the aft portion simply drifted away. For a second Captain Bryan and Fleming gazed in horror at the scene. They could already judge the sequence of tragedy. The stern would go down quickly; the larger forepart of the ship would last only a little longer.

"Abandon ship," Captain Bryan said, as if to himself.

First mate Fleming tossed the radio phone away. It was no longer useful; the breakup of the ship had severed the power cables. He had been so busy in the few minutes of terror during which the ship broke in half that he had not found a life jacket. A seaman handed him a ring buoy instead but he never made use of it. Just then the forepart of the ship lurched and rolled over. It was at that moment that most of the crew were washed into the raging waters. Fleming, losing his grip on the ring buoy, was one of them. Watchman Frank Mayes, who had reached the deck from the conveyor room by that time, was another.

Fleming and Mayes were fortunate. Struggling against towering swells to keep their heads above water, they both saw a glimmer of hope in an orange-colored raft

supported by oil drums that had broken away from the
Bradley and was floating a few feet away. It was almost
dark now, and they did not dare let the raft get away. With
desperate strokes they managed to swim to the raft, and,
half-exhausted, they hauled themselves aboard.

The scene in the water around them was nightmarish.
Crew members were scattered all around the sinking
Bradley, trying frantically to stay alive in the turbulent
waters. There were ring buoys floating about with lights
attached, but they did little to brighten the gathering
darkness, lending only an eerie glow to the scene. Men in
the water were hollering to each other, but it was a
useless gesture for it seemed impossible that any of them
could remain afloat for long. The night was cold, the
waters icy, and the chances of survival stood almost at
zero.

Most of the crew members remained alive long enough
to see their ship disappear. The aft section went first,
sinking within a couple of minutes. As she plunged to her
grave, the water swept over the boilers, setting off a
violent explosion. Only a minute or two later the forepart
also went down.

The proud and gallant *Carl D. Bradley*—thought to be
virtually unsinkable—had succumbed to the violence of
the early winter storm and had gone down in 330 feet of
water 47 miles northwest of Charlevoix, Michigan.

The closest ship to the tragedy was the *Christian
Satori*, a German freighter whose skipper was Captain
Muller. The *Christian Sartori* was four miles distant from
the *Bradley* and, when Captain Muller picked up the
Mayday call and the position of the stricken ship, he
headed at top speed to the scene. As he approached he
saw red flares lighting the waters briefly, apparently set
off by some of the *Bradley*'s crew, but by the time the
Christian Sartori actually arrived at the spot where the

Bradley had gone down, there were no signs of crew members in the water.

For several hours the German ship played its search-lights over the heaving waters. Finally, reluctantly, Captain Muller made a report over his radio.

"I believe all hands are lost. No lifeboats are visible."

This dour pronouncement did not discourage other rescue attempts. The *Bradley*'s distress signal had been picked up by several Coast Guard stations. Although the storm was one of the worst ever to roll over Lake Michigan (Captain Muller described it by saying, "In six years of sailing the Great Lakes, I have never seen such rough waters."), a 36-foot lifeboat put out from the Charlevoix Coast Guard station in an attempt to reach the scene of the disaster. But it was forced back after failing to make headway against the towering waves.

Next the U.S. Coast Guard cutter *Sundew* made an attempt and finally reached the area of the tragedy. There the Coast Guardsmen found the *Hollyhock*, out of Sturgeon Bay, Wisconsin, already searching the waters. There was also a Coast Guard helicopter overhead, dropping flares to light the blackness of the night. But there was no sign of life.

It was now 11:00 P.M. The storm was still raging, the waves were monstrous, the *Bradley* was at the bottom of the lake. There seemed no possibility that anyone had survived. Even if someone had, it was almost impossible to find the bobbing heads of survivors in the inky blackness around them.

Although the casualty list at that time was not known, thirty-one men had met death shortly after the *Bradley* went down. But four were still alive. Two were first mate Elmer Fleming and watchman Frank Mayes, both of whom had miraculously found the ship's raft in the howling storm. With them on the raft were deckhands Gary Strzelecki and Dennis Meredith. The air temperature was 20 degrees above zero, the water temperature about 30.

With no protection against the pitiless elements, with waves washing over the flimsy raft again and again, could these four men survive until daylight when they might be spotted by rescuers? It seemed highly unlikely.

Fleming and Mayes had, of course, reached the raft first and watched the agonizing death of the *Bradley* from their perilous position. A few minutes later they had observed Meredith and Strzelecki in the water and had pulled them aboard. Before darkness closed in completely they saw others in the water, but were unable to help them. All the four men could do was look on in horror as their companions floated out of sight, unable to swim against the savage waves to reach the raft. Finally, after the hideous night closed over them, the hollering of crew members ceased, and they could neither see nor hear any sign of life. There was silence, interrupted only by the howling of the tempest that surged around them.

Wet, exhausted, cold, the four men huddled together at the center of the ten-by-eight raft for whatever warmth their own bodies would supply. The raft pitched crazily in the storm, riding up one huge swell after another, dropping into shallows that seemed bottomless, and it took all the strength in their arms and legs to keep from being swept from their storm-tossed refuge.

At times it did not seem that the raft would hold together. So flimsy a craft in such raging waters seemed inevitably doomed.

"If we can keep afloat until morning," Mayes calculated, "we'll be rescued. By daylight boats and planes will be searching for us."

That was the problem, keeping afloat until daylight.

That would mean twelve hours or more of exposure to the frigid waters that washed over them and the biting chill of the night. Was it possible to stay alive that long?

First mate Fleming didn't want to chance survival through the night if there was any possibility of rescue sooner. The raft's oars had been lost but there was a hatch that contained survival gear including flares, and Fleming kept firing them into the Stygian blackness of the night, hoping a ship coming to rescue them would see the lights. At last he was down to the final flare.

"I'll save this one," he said practically, "until we see a Coast Guard cutter or some other rescue ship close by. Then I'll set it off."

This was good common sense, but in this case it did not work. An hour or so later the right moment came when something black and big loomed in the darkness. It was the German ship, *Christian Sartori*.

"It's a ship!" Mayes cried. "Fire the flare!"

But Fleming found that the flare was inoperative. The waves, crashing over the raft, had so moistened it that it would not work. "First I couldn't get it open," Fleming said later. "I tore at it and used my teeth. Then it wouldn't ignite."

The big black ship went by in the darkness, never sighting them with her sweeping searchlights and never hearing the shouts of the men over the howling noise of the storm. It seemed that their last hope of rescue before morning was gone.

The miserable foursome again crowded together like lost and frightened children. The raft was tossing about wildly, and there was constant danger that someone might slip off into the lake. Soon the four survivors noticed that the intense cold was as much an enemy as the rolling waves. They observed a numbness in their hands and feet. Their faces became raw and red as the waters and the winds assailed them. And the same thought occurred to all of them: If our hands become numb we will no longer be able to hold on.

Strzelecki proved to be the most inspiring of the four stranded men. For hours he kept encouraging the others not to give up. He would try to pierce the darkness in his search for the next wave to hit the raft, and he'd say, "Here comes a big one, fellows! Let's get set!" And the foursome would cling to the raft, gritting their teeth as the wave lifted them without effort and disdainfully threw them back into the water from its crest.

The ordeal went on—one hour, two, three. The raft bobbed like a cork in the unruly waters. At one point the eagle-eyed Strzelecki saw a light in the brooding sky.

"It's an airplane!" he shouted. "They're out searching for us. They'll find us! Hang on, fellows!"

And the foursome would hang on tighter, hoping, praying that rescue would come soon.

Then something happened that almost put a tragic end to their saga of courage. A huge, sky-high wave—perhaps twenty feet high—lifted the raft and flipped it completely over. The four men were dumped into the churning lake and the raft, upside-down, landed several yards away!

It was almost impossible to find the raft again in the blue-black darkness. When it was finally sighted it seemed improbable that they could regain possession of it. Yet they knew they had to. They could not survive for long in the freezing waters, and their only hope was the raft.

The knowledge that they must get back to the raft gave them super strength. Swimming against the high-rolling waves, all four managed to reach the raft and climb aboard again, and when they had regained their position they lay exhausted on the wooden planks, barely able to move.

Finally Fleming roused himself from approaching

lethargy. "Don't go to sleep men," he pleaded. "Don't go to sleep or you're a goner!"

The wetness of the men increased their suffering from the cold. Meredith, in worse shape than the other three, was shivering and seemed on the verge of unconsciousness. Fleming put his arms around him and shook him gently.

"Don't go to sleep," he said again. "Once you go to sleep you're gone."

Meredith did not reply. He did not move. The three men looked furtively at each other.

"Let's count to make sure we don't go to sleep," Fleming suggested.

They started to count in unison. "One . . . two . . . three . . . four . . . " Three voices only. Meredith remained quiet. Then they began to talk in reassuring terms to each other, trying not only to keep awake but to encourage each other to hang on grimly.

"There'll be all kinds of search parties out."

"They're bound to find us."

"Any time now. It won't take long."

But they knew it would take long. Probably until morning.

The night wore on.

Several more times the four men were either washed off the raft by a wave or the raft was upset, spilling them into icy water. Once, when this happened, Dennis Meredith failed to return. The others, who had managed to scramble back to the raft, scanned the dark waves about them, but they never saw him again.

All night long the three seamen rode the raft. It was so cold that ice formed on their clothing and in their hair. This alarmed them as much as anything.

"We could stay on the raft all night and still freeze to death," one of them said.

This thought plagued the minds of the three men, and finally Strzelecki, who had been so instrumental in keeping the hopes of the survivors alive, broke under the strain. Exposure, exhaustion, and shock had taken its toll. A wild look came into his eyes, and he rose to his feet, obviously intending to jump overboard.

Both Fleming and Mayes tried to stop him, but they were too weak to hold him, and Strzelecki leaped into the water and went down. It was now two men against the storm. Two men praying for rescue as soon as daylight came.

At last, after what seemed an endless night, the first gray streaks of dawn appeared. The sky brightened slowly, and a ghostly light spread over the water. In the distance they saw the murky outline of High Island, one of the Beaver Island archipelago. They estimated they were about 20 miles from where the *Bradley* had gone down.

Calculating the drift of the raft and the distance to High Island, Fleming and Mayes decided they had a good chance of landing there. But it wasn't necessary. Shortly after daylight a Coast Guard helicopter spotted the two men floating on the bone-chilling lake and radioed the Coast Guard cutter *Sundew*. The cutter raced to the scene and hauled the two wet, half-frozen men aboard. Within minutes the helicopter picked them up and sped them to a hospital on the mainland. At 9:07 A.M. the *Sundew* flashed a cryptic message: "Picked up two survivors on raft 5.25 miles from Gull Island."

The two men had been on the raft for fourteen and a half hours, battling valiantly against death in frigid temperatures and numbing waters! There were no other survivors. Thirty-three members of the *Bradley*'s crew had perished in the disaster. About half of the bodies were eventually recovered; the others were lost.

A few days later an interview with the two survivors at the hospital revealed some interesting sidelights into what men think about when death is near. Mayes, a Catholic, was asked if he prayed and if he used the Our Father, the Hail Mary, or the Apostles' Creed.

> Oh, sure, all of those, but another one in particular. It's from the Gospel—"Ask in my Father's name, and you shall receive." Christ said it. I don't know where, or who he was talking to, but out there on the raft I used that prayer. I asked to be spared to help the others and my family. I asked and I received.

Fleming, a Presbyterian, was asked the same question and gave this reflective answer.

> I couldn't tell you any special prayer. The mysteries of religion are beyond me. You've just got to believe and that's it. When they say two wives' prayers were answered, what about the other thirty-three? Those other fellows in the water prayed just as hard as us, and their wives prayed all night, same as ours. Why my prayers and Frank's were answered is something we'll never understand. It's like my wife had to tell our son when the report came in that the *Bradley* was sunk. She told him, "Your father might never come home, Douglas, but you've got to remember we're not waiting alone."

Both Fleming and Mayes recovered from their ordeal in a short time. Both men were bruised by their horrendous raft ride, but Fleming seemed to be in worse shape. Both his knees and shins were black and blue from the pummeling they had received.

> I was whipped to the bone on that raft. Fighting on those slats all night is no bargain, but you don't feel it then. You can scrape the meat right off your legs trying to get back on that raft and you don't even feel it.

Mayes had only one bruise on his legs, but he complained of having no feeling in his feet. "There's just a tingle in my toes," he said.

Asked if they were confident of rescue, Mayes said, "We knew the Coast Guard would be around if we could make it to daylight."

"Yes," Fleming put in. "We're steamboat men. We know how slow it is (how long it takes). You aren't driving a car around the block out there. But when she came close, that *Sundew* looked big."

Mayes nodded and smiled.

"Big," he repeated.

That Fleming and Mayes had survived one of the most unbelievable storms in the Great Lakes history was testified to by a Coast Guardsman who summed up the situation handily.

> This storm was the worst I've ever seen on the lakes. Ocean sailors always kid us lake men about our millponds. But I'd better not hear that again. Last night was a visit to hell.

16

The Perilous Search for the *Hans Hedtoft* (1959)

T HE year was 1957; the place Copenhagen, Denmark. Augo Lynge, distinguished member of parliament from the Danish island of Greenland, stood before his colleagues and solemnly warned against the sailing of passenger vessels to Greenland in the months of January, February, and March.

"These are the most dangerous months because of icebergs and gales," he said. "It is folly to build a passenger ship designed to service Greenland during these winter months."

Since Lynge had personally experienced many rugged winters in Greenland, his words should have had considerable weight. But they fell on unheeding ears. Johannes Kjaerbock, Minister of Greenland, insisted that it was absolutely necessary to keep Greenland open the entire year to sea traffic, and he scoffingly minimized the danger.

It was a time when the Danish Government was just beginning work on an Arctic passenger-cargo ship to be called the *Hans Hedtoft,* named in honor of a notable Prime Minister of Denmark. Her owner was Denmark's Ministry of Greenland, and she would be managed by the Royal Greenland Trade Department. It would take two years of work until the vessel was finished and she was fit with all the paraphernalia necessary to insure her safety in high seas and iceberg-dotted waters. During the entire time of her construction, the building of the *Hans Hedtoft* was to be a much-debated subject that was to occupy both the government and the people of Denmark.

As the ship began to take shape, the argument over its construction raged unendingly. Some supporters of the project contended it was the government's responsibility to operate shipping to Greenland, and therefore the ship had to be built. Others countered that this was a foolish argument of no merit. Those who wanted to see the *Hans Hedtoft* born felt certain that a ship could be constructed that was stout and seaworthy enough to withstand the violent winter storms and menacing bergs. Others said it was impossible to expect any ship to traverse the dangerous waters around Greenland in safety. To support their argument they cited the destruction of the "unsinkable" *Titanic* after it struck an iceberg in 1912—on a route much farther south than the *Hans Hedtoft* was expected to sail.

As one man put it, "The route laid out for the *Hans Hedtoft* is right up there where the big bergs are born—a very dangerous situation."

Nevertheless, the ship was built. When she was finished she appeared, indeed, to be a vessel constructed with emphasis on ruggedness and durability. The *Hans Hedtoft* weighed 2,800 gross tons, measured 288 feet from bow to stern, and was reported to be fitted with every device known to assure safe navigation in treacherous northern waters. She was provided with a double steel bottom, a heavily armored bow and stern, and had seven water-tight compartments.

The Danish Government made a point of explaining that, in the unlikely event of a serious emergency, the *Hans Hedtoft* was well equipped to take care of her passengers. She carried three lifeboats made of light metal alloy, several rubber dinghies or life rafts, and a motor launch. Each of these was furnished with emergency hand-operated radio transmitters that broadcast on the 600-meter band at 500 kilocycles.

If ever a ship was ready for rugged duty, the *Hans Hedtoft* seemed to be the one.

In January, 1959, the *Hans Hedtoft* sailed from Copenhagen on her maiden run. She was under the command of Captain P. L. Rasmussen, a thin hawk-faced skipper of 58 years who had sailed in Arctic seas all of his adult life and was one of the most respected of his country's famous polar seamen. The ship carried fifty-five passengers and a crew of forty.

The *Hans Hedtoft's* destination on the outward leg of her initial journey was Godthaab, the capital of Greenland. She was then scheduled to return home, bringing with her an equivalent number of passengers and a hold full of salted and frozen fish from the far north to delight the taste buds of Copenhageners.

The route taken by the *Hans Hedtoft* was far to the north of all regular shipping lanes, but on her first crossing she had little trouble sailing the frigid ice-choked waters. Captain Rasmussen guided her around the southern tip of Greenland and up the western coast of the huge island with an expertness derived from long experience. Docking at Godthaab, he disembarked his passengers and substituted fifty-five others, filled his hold with iced fish, and was ready to depart for Copenhagen on the second half of his maiden run.

Among the passengers, this time, was Augo Lynge, the man who had tried two years before to point out the danger inherent in a ship sailing Greenland waters during the perilous winter months.

The voyage from Copenhagen to Godthaab had been a comparatively easy one as Arctic travel goes. But the return journey began on a different note. No sooner had the *Hans Hedtoft* left the Godthaab harbor and sailed south than she was beset by rough weather. Waves ten to fifteen feet high, churned up by raw Arctic winds, had the ship rolling in heavy seas. At times she rolled from port to starboard and back again; at others her bow rose on the crest of a huge swell, then "bottomed out" as she plunged bow-first into the shallows that preceded the next wave. Before long she was an ice-coated ship, glistening with an eerie whiteness as she laboriously made her way against biting winds and an angry sea.

But the intrepid Captain Rasmussen had known such conditions before, and he deftly piloted the *Hans Hedtoft* down the rugged western coast of Greenland, made the turn east at the southern tip of the island, and headed with confidence toward the open sea.

As she made the turn a blinding snowstorm descended on the *Hans Hedtoft*, and visibility became badly restricted. To add to the problem, a heavy fog settled over the area, and Captain Rasmussen reduced his speed and proceeded with due caution. Although the ship was rolling, the skipper was certain she was in no danger. She was built to weather heavy seas. The only danger was the presence of icebergs, but this did not dismay the captain. Captain Rasmussen was an experienced polar skipper who could "smell" the cold breath of an iceberg before he could see it. He felt certain that he could pick his way through any ice field he might happen upon. He had done it before, and he could do it again.

The passengers, however, were less certain that the

journey was a safe one. Some were so seasick that they cared little whether the voyage ended in success or disaster. Others were apprehensive as the ship rolled frighteningly—particularly Augo Lynge, who knew something of the sea and the savagery of a Greenland winter.

The *Hans Hedtoft* was thirty-seven miles south of Cape Farvel [Farewell], the southernmost point of the huge Danish island, when disaster struck. Suddenly, out of a shroud of fog and undetected by the ship's radar, a mammoth iceberg loomed. It was so close to the ship that a collision could not be avoided. There was a crunch as the *Hans Hedtoft* struck the berg, and then settled back into the water, mortally wounded.

The time of the crash was approximately 11:30 A.M. on January 30, 1959.

The world did not know of the calamity until about noon when the *Hans Hedtoft* tapped out its first brief message by radio, giving the ship's position and describing the accident simply as "collision with an iceberg." But her second message, only a few minutes later, was more informative—and more chilling. It said, again very laconically, "We are filling fast."

Later in the day a third message crackled over the air. "We are taking a lot of water in the engine room," it said.

There exists today no knowledge of what was happening on board the sinking *Hans Hedtoft* while the messages of impending disaster were being reported by radio. But one can surmise from the condition of the weather and the ship what was taking place. It seems obvious that there was no way out for the passengers and crew of the Danish ship. She was rolling in waves twenty feet high. Lowering the three lifeboats in such heavy seas was equivalent to committing suicide. Even had they been lowered—and it is possible a desperate attempt was made—they were sure to be swamped or capsized when they hit the water. Neither was there any possibility of the passengers jumping overboard with life preservers in the hope that they would be pulled out of the sea by another ship. First of all, the *Hans Hedtoft's* position north of normal shipping lanes made it highly unlikely that another ship could reach her in time. And second, the waters were so cold that a human being cast into them could live no longer than a minute.

With such hopeless odds confronting them, the passengers must have been aware of how close they were to death. One can only guess what Augo Lynge was thinking. He had fought against the building of the ship, had tried to persuade Denmark's Parliament to abandon the idea of sending passengers into the wild and churning cauldron of ice that virtually blocked access to Greenland ports in winter, but he had been ignored. Now his own death was about to emphasize the correctness of his views.

Brief messages came from the *Hans Hedtoft* for several hours during her ordeal, never describing the conditions aboard but giving only factual information about the ship's condition. The last message came at 3:55 P.M. It said, "Slowly sinking. Need immediate assistance."

That was all. Following the request for assistance the radio messages stopped. The failure of the radio was the most ominous message of all.

Had the *Hans Hedtoft* gone down?

The search for the *Hans Hedtoft* and any possible survivors was one of the most dangerous sea adventures ever undertaken. The stubborn determination exhibited by the U.S. Coast Guard personnel and other seamen in their efforts to locate survivors, despite the cruelty of the weather, marks it as one of the most dramatic search attempts in the annals of the sea.

At the time that the *Hans Hedtoft* struck the iceberg

there was only one other ship in the general vicinity. She was the 650-ton German trawler *Johannes Kruess*, fishing the waters off the southern tip of Greenland. She, too, had been fighting high seas and fog, not to mention floating bergs. Her captain was about to return to port when he received the first message from the *Hans Hedtoft* shortly after 11:30 A.M. Dropping her plan to return to the safety of port, the *Johannes Kruess* set out to locate the stricken ship immediately. At top speed she traveled toward the position given by the *Hans Hedtoft* in her broadcast—a fearful risk in itself. Blinded by the fog and chopping her way through heavy swells whipped up by gale winds, the little trawler was in constant danger of hitting an iceberg herself. But the call for assistance at sea is not a signal a ship's captain can ignore, and the intrepid trawler battled its way against the elements to reach the position of the endangered ship as darkness was closing in. When she arrived, she found no sign of the *Hans Hedtoft*.

During the trip to the scene of the disaster the *Johannes Kruess* was in radio contact with several locations. She informed the Royal Canadian Air Force Rescue Headquarters at Halifax, Nova Scotia, that she was in the area of the wreck but could find no evidence of what had happened to the *Hans Hedtoft*. She was also in touch with the U.S. Coast Guard cutter *Campbell*, some 280 miles southwest of the sinking ship's reported position. The *Campbell* at once headed into the maelstrom of violent weather to help locate the Danish passenger ship.

When the U.S. Coast Guard Rescue Coordination Center on the southern tip of Manhattan heard of the plight of the *Hans Hedtoft* immediate action was taken to coordinate the rescue attempts of all ships in the area. First, the position of the vessel in distress was marked by a yellow triangle on a monstrous map of the north Atlantic. Then Coast Guardsmen consulted an electronic machine that gave them the positions of other ships that might be of help. Noting that their own cutter *Campbell* was closest to the trouble area, they radioed a "proceed and assist" order, only to learn that the cutter was already on the way. The Center sent messages out to all ships close enough to be of some help—coast guard cutters, freighters, passenger ships—although they were comparatively few in number. They had no authority, of course, to demand that merchant ships take part in the rescue operations, but it was generally assumed that any ship so notified would obey the rules of the sea and attempt to locate the *Hans Hedtoft*.

Meanwhile, planes were taking to the air, daring the savage storm off the southern tip of Greenland to impede them. A U.S. Air Force radar picket plane joined the search, taking off from Argentia, Newfoundland, for the 750-mile three-hour flight to the scene. A U.S. Navy Super-Constellation also headed for the area, along with a Royal Canadian Air Force Lancaster.

From the planes, as they reached the scene, came a fearful report. Lying northeast-southwest along the edge of the *Hans Hedtoft*'s position when she struck the iceberg was a mammoth field of ice a half mile wide and forty miles long. It represented a formidable barrier for ships attempting to reach the scene of tragedy.

The Coast Guard cutter *Campbell*—closest ship to the scene with the exception of the *Johannes Kruess*—chopped its way through rolling seas, hoping to reach the disaster scene no later than noon the next day. She was under the command of Captain Frederick J. Scheiber, an experienced skipper who had served in the Greenland ice patrol during World War II. Undaunted by the possible danger to his own ship, he intended to travel as fast as possible all night long to reach the position given by the *Hans Hedtoft* before her radio went dead.

Throughout the night the *Campbell* rolled, climbed waves, plunged, battling fiercely against heavy winds, high seas, and impenetrable darkness. Even as she did so, Captain Scheiber doubted, from the reports he received from the trawler, that there was any chance to rescue anyone from the Danish ship. He was already certain that the *Hans Hedtoft* had gone down with all hands. But on the bare hope, the slight expectancy, that someone might still be alive in a gale-battered lifeboat, he was willing to risk his ship to reach them.

At the scene of the collision the *Johannes Kruess* was in just as much danger as she circled an eight-square mile area in a vain hope that she might stumble either upon the *Hans Hedtoft* still afloat or wreckage that would prove her demise. But finally she sent a message to the *Campbell*.

"We have searched, nothing found or seen, no lights or lifeboats or ship," it said. "Plenty of ice from the northwest and we are becoming ice-bound." There was a moment's hesitation and then, "We must go. It is dangerous for the ship, and we can do no more."

When the *Campbell* returned to the scene at noon the next day, visibility was estimated at half a mile. Captain Scheiber circled the area for several hours. Then, to his surprise, the *Johannes Kruess* returned to aid in the search. Another German vessel, the motor ship *Poseidon*, also arrived at the scene to join the search.

It was no pleasure cruise for any of them. A howling wind whipped snow over the area. Twenty foot waves crashed around and over the searching ships. It was dangerous work, performed under the worst of conditions, and the dedication of the seamen to their task was remarkable. Actually, everyone was convinced by this time that the search was hopeless. The area was filled with dangerous, heavy ice and the chances that any of the fifty-five passengers and forty crewmen could have escaped the *Hans Hedtoft* before she sank was slim indeed.

But still the search went on and when darkness finally closed in Captain Scheiber of the *Campbell* radioed a lengthy report on the situation the searchers faced.

> Encountering scattered heavy ice consisting of bergs, berg bits, growlers and brash [icebergs, broken ice from icebergs, low-riding chunks of glaciers and broken pack ice] plus occasional floebergs [massive hummocks of pack ice]. Concentration approximately five per square mile. Concentration building up rapidly to north near ice floe one-half mile wide and forty miles long orientation northeast by southwest reported by aircraft. The conditions making navigation throughout area very hazardous but continuing search until darkness. Have to get out tonight. Too dangerous to operate inside.

Later that night the *Campbell* reported she was standing by with the German ship *Poseidon* outside the dangerous ice area, waiting until daybreak to renew the search. A couple of Danish ships had also moved into position to take up the search when daylight neared. One of them was the 2,318-ton passenger ship *Umanak*, carrying 85 passengers of her own.

During the night, as the ships stood by, preparatory to resuming the search in the morning, a flurry of excitement gripped them. The Danish ship *Umanak* suddenly reported that she had picked up weak radio signals— possibly coming from a lifeboat equipped with a hand-operated radio. At about the same time word came from Copenhagen that weak signals were also heard by coast guard stations in Greenland.

The *Umanak* reported that the signals were scattered and irregularly spaced, indicating that an untrained operator was attempting to send distress signals on equipment he did not thoroughly understand. Two radio stations on the Greenland coast, supporting the word from Copenhagen, said they, too, had heard the feeble signals.

However, the U.S. cutter *Campbell* did not hear the signals and neither did the rescue center of the Royal Canadian Air Force at Halifax. "None of our receiving centers, ships or aircraft heard the signals," was the Air Force report.

Another rumor to support the possibility of a lifeboat in the vicinity came to light when an aircraft pilot, on returning to his base at Goose Bay, Labrador, reported that he had sighted what appeared to be a white lifeboat with a black stripe on it, although he conceded that because of poor visibility it might only have been a floating chunk of ice. The Royal Greenland Trading Company, managers of the *Hans Hedtoft*, squelched that report, however, by saying that the Danish ship's lifeboats were metal and unpainted.

The mystery of the weak radio signals was never solved, although the report from the *Umanak* and the two stations in Greenland spurred the bevy of ships waiting for daylight to renew their search. They went forth determined to look sharply for a lifeboat still floating in the churning waters.

But visibility was so poor that there was little chance to find a lifeboat even if one existed. The waves, urged on by sixty mile an hour winds, had increased to forty feet in height, making radar ineffective and diminishing maneuverability almost to zero. In addition, huge chunks of floating ice were everywhere, making the entire undertaking not only deathly hazardous but almost impossible.

Still the search continued, despite the mountainous waves, threatening ice, snow squalls, and fog. When the long day was completed the ice-shrouded ships again retreated to a safer place at night. They had found no lifeboat, no wreckage, and, of course, no sign of the *Hans Hedtoft*.

The next day the search was ended. There was no doubt by then that the *Hans Hedtoft* had gone down with all hands aboard. Wearily, weather-beaten, the rescue ships hurried for the security of nearby ports. One of the most hazardous and fearful searches in the annals of the sea was over. Even though it had ended in failure it stood out, and still does, as one of the most magnificent examples of bravery in maintaining the tradition of the sea.

The supreme irony came later, when news of the demise of the *Hans Hedtoft* with the loss of 95 persons became official. The Danish Government, which had failed to heed the advice of Augo Lynge, announced in sepulchral tones that "the whole nation is shocked by this great catastrophe." No word was mentioned, of course, that the government had been warned of impending disaster two years earlier.

Had Augo Lynge, lying at the bottom of an icy sea, been able to hear the official pronouncement, he might have shaken his head ruefully.

17

Last Voyage of
the *Lakonia* (1963)

T HE date was December 19, 1963; the place, Southampton, England. The day was cold, damp, and miserable—a typical winter day in the British Isles. Tied up at one of the many quays that service ships from all corners of the world was the 20,314-ton Greek cruise liner *Lakonia*. She was taking aboard 658 excited passengers—most of them British—all eager to exchange the English winter for the sun and warmth of Madeira and the Canary Islands. The crew numbered 383, making a total complement of 1,041 persons aboard.

Cruise passengers are normally a happy and chattering group, and those who poured aboard the *Lakonia* were no exception. Most of them had signed up for the entire two-week cruise that would take them to places with such exotic names as Madeira, Tenerife, and Las Palmas. Others were contemplating longer stays in the balmy climate of the Canaries.

The passengers ran the gamut from experienced world travelers to first-timers. There was 70-year-old Harry Knight of Stockport, England, who had traveled extensively in Europe and was determined to see as much of the world as possible in the time left to him. For others, like Mr. and Mrs. Fred Calvert, from the cold, northern town of Nelson, the trip was a necessity; they were traveling for their health. Fred Calvert was a diabetic, and his wife was nursing a hand injured in a weaving mill accident. Their doctor had prescribed rest for both of them, and Mrs. Calvert's accident compensation had made it possible for them to take the trip. Mrs. Gertrude Moore, proprietress of a London pub, was taking her third voyage on the *Lakonia*, this time accompanied by her daughter. And there were three sets of starry-eyed honeymooners taking the first cruise of their young lives. Also taking their first cruise were 34 children.

The cruise brochure had promised "absolute freedom from worry and responsibility"—and this was what lured many of the passengers. The ship was a floating palace, with soft lights and tapestry-draped lounges. There would be dancing to the ship's orchestra at night; shuffleboard, swimming, deck tennis, and relaxing in deck chairs during the day. And Christmas would be celebrated at sea—a new and thrilling experience for many.

Most of the passengers knew nothing of the *Lakonia*'s past history, or if they did they chose to ignore it. In retrospect, they should have paid closer attention, for the Greek liner had been a troubled ship almost from the beginning.

The *Lakonia* was formerly the Dutch ship *Johan van Oldenbarnevelt*, built by the Nederland Shipping Company in 1930. From the date she was placed in active service there was a chain of strange happenings aboard the ship. On her maiden voyage in 1930, with none other than Queen Wilhelmina of the Netherlands aboard, she had the ill luck to collide with another ship in the North Sea. In 1951, fire was the culprit. The *Johan van Oldenbarnevelt* sailed from Amsterdam, Holland, with almost 1,500 emigrants aboard, and six small but potentially dangerous fires broke out during the journey. Nobody ever determined how they started. A little later, on a cruise, there was an unbelievable foul-up when angry passengers found they were not given the staterooms they had booked, that work on the ship was still going on when she sailed, and that tools were strewn haphazardly around public rooms. The result of this fiasco was that her owners had to refund at least a third of the fares collected.

In 1962 the troubled ship was put up for sale and purchased by the Ormos Shipping Company, Ltd., of London, a Greek firm. The Greek owners placed the ship in drydock in an Italian shipyard and ordered it completely overhauled and refitted. When the work was done the ship was renamed the *Lakonia* and placed in service out of Southampton. She was scheduled to make cruises to various sunny climes as part of a year-round service from that port.

Before the *Lakonia* sailed on December 19, the crew participated in a boat and fire drill, as required by marine law. Captain Daniel Jones, of the British Sea Transport Department, had inspectors aboard, and they reported that the drills met the requirements of the International Convention for the Safety of Life at Sea and had proceeded with precision and smoothness. Since the *Lakonia* carried a Greek certificate of seaworthiness, the British had no authority to conduct a physical inspection of the ship.

On the first day after sailing a boat drill was held for the passengers—a routine procedure. With everything in order and the passengers supposedly informed on what to do in case of an emergency, the *Lakonia* clipped along at 17 knots. On December 21 she was in the Bay of Biscay, off the coasts of Spain and France, in fairly rough water with an east wind blowing off the Continent. By the next day the weather had improved, and a warm sun began to provide the suntans that the British passengers hoped to get as a souvenir of their journey.

Late in the evening of December 22, the *Lakonia* was in calm seas, again slashing a silvery path through the water at 17 knots. In the ship's dimly-lit lounge dancing couples crowded the floor, swaying gracefully to the strains of the ship's orchestra. Many passengers had already retired to their staterooms and were either asleep or preparing for bed. Others strolled the decks, savoring the warm evening and gazing at the silver streak the moon etched in the water.

At exactly 11:00 P.M. an alert steward, passing the closed barber shop, noticed a wisp of smoke seeping from beneath the door. Acting quickly, he opened the door and fell back as a red-orange tongue of flame darted toward him. Rushing for help, he noticed that the flames had immediately ignited the hallway and were racing down the passageway toward the staterooms.

At almost the same instant the skipper of the *Lakonia*, Captain M. N. Zarbis, sitting in the main saloon, smelled smoke and bolted from the room. A few seconds later the ship's alarm sounded.

A ship's alarm, ringing suddenly and without warning, is a frightening thing, and the passengers reacted with dismay and confusion. Some stayed where they were, wondering what to do. Many, anticipating that an emergency was at hand, rushed to their staterooms to get life preservers. Others, attempting to go to their cabins, found themselves already cut off by flames. Shouts from men and screams from women mingled in the lounge with the orchestra's music. The musicians doggedly kept playing in an attempt to calm the crowd.

In the radio room the duty officer, Alexis Kalogridis, was busy sending Christmas greetings to far away places for the passengers. Suddenly a message from the bridge warned him: "We are on fire. Start emergency procedure at once."

Kalogridis discarded the Christmas messages and went into immediate action. He promptly sent out the recognized distress signal—a dash repeated at four second intervals. This signal would assure that any ship in the vicinity would stand by for further instructions. Then he tapped out the information that sent chills through radio operators on a host of nearby ships.

"SOS. SOS. This is the *Lakonia*. We are on fire. Request immediate assistance."

This was followed by the position of the ship: "Latitude 35 degrees north; Longitude 24 degrees west."

Half an hour later the message changed, and various ships steaming toward the imperiled *Lakonia* in answer to her call picked it up.

"We are leaving the ship. Please immediately give us assistance. Please help us."

At 12:22 A.M. came the final message. "SOS from *Lakonia* last time. I cannot stay any more in the wireless station. We are leaving the ship. Please immediate assistance. Please help."

While Kalogridis was tapping out these frantic messages, the lifeboat deck was a scene of complete confusion. People in all stages of dress were either milling around aimlessly or attempting to get into lifeboats. Some, awakened in their staterooms by the alarm, were in their pajamas. Others, coming from the dance in the lounge, wore evening clothes. Some of the men were dressed impeccably in tuxedos, the women in long glittering evening gowns.

In the meantime, there was feverish activity as shore stations along the coasts of Europe and northern Africa picked up the distress signals of the *Lakonia* and re-broadcast them to ships over an immense area. There were five ships within 100 miles of the Greek liner, others considerably outside that range, but within minutes of receiving the signals all were steaming through the black night toward the disaster scene. The U.S. Coast Guard was alerted, and the cutter *Mackinac*, running between Newfoundland and the Azores, headed for the *Lakonia* along with four others. U.S. Air Rescue units took off from the Azores, as well as from Reinstein, Germany and Madrid, Spain. All freighters in the well-traveled shipping lane converged on the blazing pleasure ship.

A rising wind, but not a dangerous one, was ruffling the waters around the *Lakonia* when the first rescue ship arrived on the scene. She was the 5,000-ton British ship *Montcalm*, and she was followed in short order by the Argentine ship *Salta* and the British liner *Stratheden*. Still at a distance but headed toward the *Lakonia* were the German tanker *Gertrud Frizen*, the Pakistan ship *Mehdi*, the British aircraft carrier H.M.S. *Centaur*, the American liners *Rio Grande* and *Independence*, and the Belgian ship *Charlesville*. In the air were U.S. C-54s and British Shackletons, as well as other aircraft. On shore medical facilities were being readied at places like Madeira, the Canary Islands, Gibraltar, and Rabat and Casablanca in Morocco.

As the rescue ships rushed toward the stricken liner, those on board the *Lakonia* were hustled into lifeboats. The flames and smoke were spreading rapidly over the ship, and had reached such proportions that it was impossible to lower four of the lifeboats because of the pressing heat. Some passengers, despairing of ever reaching a lifeboat before the entire ship was engulfed in flames, leaped overboard, preferring to take their chances in the water with lifejackets on. But the sea was cold, and it was a question of how long they could stay alive in the water. There was difficulty after some of the boats had been lowered, too. Several were swamped in swells and one boat almost crashed down on top of another.

When the *Montcalm* arrived her captain immediately commanded that searchlights be played over the water in an effort to locate survivors either in boats or in the water. They found many and hauled them aboard. The other ships moved in, adding the beams from their searchlights—and they too pulled survivors from the water.

Toward daylight a radio message came from the *Montcalm*: "We have taken 240 aboard, along with 12 dead." The *Stratheden* reported: "We have rescued 300."

As morning finally brightened the sky, the plight of the *Lakonia* could best be seen from the air. Pilots of the rescue planes saw the ship burning from the bow almost to the stern. On the aft part of the ship, which had not yet been swept by the flames, a miserable group of about 100 people—passengers and crew—were huddled, determined to stay with the ship as long as they could. With them was Captain Zarbis, pacing the deck with tears of frustration coursing down his ruddy cheeks.

At last, as the raging fire crept closer to the stern, the passengers and crew were forced to jump overboard. Some were picked up by lifeboats, others drowned.

Captain Zarbis, with the heat of the flames hot on his neck, was the last to leave the doomed liner.

By this time most of those lucky enough to get into lifeboats had been picked up by the rescue ships. The eighteen ships clustered around the blazing *Lakonia* were picking up individuals who had remained undiscovered during the dark hours but had managed to survive the ordeal in lifejackets. Some, however, had perished. Their bodies floated grotesquely in the water, lifejackets still in place over evening gowns and tuxedos. One airman said later, "I saw a small baby lying alone in a lifejacket made for a man. She was dead, and it made me feel sick."

On Christmas Eve the search for survivors ended, and on Christmas Day those saved from the fire-ravaged *Lakonia* reached land. Those on the *Stratheden* debarked at Funchal, Madeira. They were a sorry lot. Most of them were dazed and hollow-eyed by their horrifying experience. Some wept as they once again placed their feet on solid ground. Women in nightgowns, with ship's blankets wrapped around them, stumbled ashore. Many bore scrapes and bruises from lurching lifeboats. A few were carried ashore on stretchers.

Other passengers, in similar condition, were taken to Casablanca by the *Montcalm, Charlesville*, and *Mehdi*. All showed signs of shock and exhaustion. The Moroccan government offered hotel rooms for those who were uninjured and provided air transportation for those who wanted to go back to England.

An ironic note occurred when survivors at Funchal were told that another Greek Line ship, the *Arkadia*, would pick them up and take them back to Southampton. Most of them refused to board another Greek liner.

When, at last, the rescue operation was completed, the final count was set at 155 dead. Out of a combined total of 1,041 passengers and crew, 886 had been saved in one of the most extensive rescue operations of modern times.

But that was not the end of the drama. For days following the tragedy a series of bitter accusations and stout denials made the front pages of the world's newspapers. Passengers accused the Greek crew of ineptness and even desertion in the face of peril; the crew denied vehemently that there was any cause for complaint. Each accused the other of panic.

A British engineer who was traveling on the *Lakonia* made his opinion known immediately upon arrival at Funchal. "There was unpardonable confusion of orders and counter orders," he said. "The crew at one end of the ship didn't know what was happening at the other end."

Another man spoke angrily of the "shocking lack of experience of the crew." He said, "The passengers actually had to take charge when we abandoned ship. They showed more ingenuity and calmness than the crew did."

Many passengers accused the crew of being awkward in the lowering of the lifeboats, saying that two were overturned with some of the occupants lost because of inefficiency on the part of the Greek crew. "They didn't even fill them up," was the charge of Ian Hargis of London. "I saw lifeboats designed to hold seventy-five people pulling away from the ship with only twenty people in them."

Other passengers complained that in the panic that followed discovery of the fire, the crew failed to direct the passengers to the proper lifeboat stations. They said that members of the crew, when questioned by English-speaking passengers, invariably replied in Greek, adding to the chaos and confusion that was evident everywhere.

Some bedraggled passengers reported that several of the lifeboats were without bungs for the drain holes that are left open when the boats are in davits. As a result, frantic bailing went on in the boats until the rescue ships lifted them from the water.

One of the worse accusations came from passengers who charged that Greek seamen, in a state of complete panic, fought with the passengers for places in the lifeboats.

"I owe my life to a lifejacket," said Mrs. Elizabeth Taylor, a 63-year-old British woman. "I could not get into a lifeboat. The stewards got into them."

"The fire alarm was so weak that it sounded like someone calling the waiter to ask for tea," said Albert Neal Spiller, of Torquay, England. "There was no panic among the passengers. The crew appeared to be the panicky ones."

One woman accused a member of the crew of taking advantage of the fire to loot her stateroom. A man said he had to plead with the crew to let his wife get into a lifeboat, and further complained that it took thirty minutes to lower one boat because it was rusted to its davits. He supported the woman who had charged the crewman with looting by observing that he saw one Greek crewman attempting to sell jewelry that was "obviously looted from a cabin" to survivors on Madeira.

Still another survivor summed up the situation with a comment that, when the fire alarm sounded, "there was complete panic everywhere. There was no attempt by the crew to help people. We were left to take our chances. I don't believe," he said, "that one life need have been lost."

Even those who successfully made the lifeboats had complaints. One passenger said that the Greek crew didn't seem to know what to do when they were in the lifeboat and attempted to take the rescued people back to the burning ship. He claimed that the passengers took over the lifeboat and remained in the water seven hours until the *Salta* picked them up. "And when she did," he remarked, "that Greek crew was the first up the ladder lowered for us!"

One woman even accused crew members of being drunk at the time of crisis.

Naturally, all these allegations were promptly denied by Captain Zarbis and other officers. Telephoning London from Santa Cruz de Tenerife, the captain said, "There was no panic aboard my ship, neither with the crew nor the passengers. And there was no drunkenness. I was the one who gave the order to abandon ship. It was my duty to do so." When asked about statements that the crew climbed into the lifeboats before the passengers, he said, "That was not the case at all."

But one crew member, Josef Kronschnabl, said briefly that "the operation was very disorganized. That is all I can say for now."

While this seething argument was going on, the fate of the *Lakonia*, itself, was in doubt. She lay burning as the Norwegian salvage ship *Herkules* and the Dutch tug *Polzee* made an effort to tow her into Gibraltar. They managed to get the charred and burning hulk of the *Lakonia* in tow, but about 250 miles from Gibraltar the ship went down in 2,000 fathoms of water—thereby frustrating a team of experts who were headed for Gibraltar to determine, if possible, the exact cause of the fire.

On December 29 a preliminary investigation into the fire was begun in Athens, Greece. Commander Nestor Phokas, head of the Athens Central Harbor Police Department, presided over the inquiry, and his report was slated to go to the Greek Merchant Marine Minister, Polychronis Polychronides, who would be charged with deciding if the case should be referred to the Commission of Maritime Accidents. At the preliminary inquiry Captain Zarbis and 47 crew members were closely questioned. Captain Zarbis defended the action of his crew, saying they had performed excellently. Crew members steadfastly denied that there was any panic at any time.

Several cases of bravery among crew members were cited to support the contention that the crew was faultless. Dimos Zilakos, the ship's accountant, was given credit for saving an old lady and a small child from a burning stateroom. Panayiotis Mantikos, a seaman, saved three elderly passengers by hooking up rope ladders while his own life was in danger. Ioannis Mimskikokos, a steward, saved women and children from staterooms and, with ropes, helped elderly passengers through portholes without regard for his own safety.

One damning bit of evidence emerged from the inquiry, however. It was found that in the refitting of the *Lakonia* prior to the cruise, she was not fitted with automatic water sprinklers in case of fire. Instead, she was fitted only with a series of fuses that triggered alarms when the temperature rose too high—but not with devices to quench the flames automatically.

When all testimony was taken, the facts were presented to the Greek Merchant Marine Ministry. After careful study of all reports, the Ministry decided that the "crew acted faultlessly and in accordance with Greek tradition" and that "the complaints of passengers were exaggerated as a result of panic."

Thus the case of the *Lakonia*'s last voyage was closed, with passengers and crew still in disagreement. The true story of the burning of the Greek liner remains shrouded in mystery.